7·99

# *REFRESHED BY THE WORD*

## CYCLE C

*by*
*John E. O'Brien*

GW00494423

PAULIST PRESS
New York / Mahwah

*Cover design by James F. Brisson*

All scripture quotations are from The New American Bible with The Revised Book of Psalms and The Revised New Testament. Minor adaptations have been made in some passages to incorporate more inclusive language.

Nihil Obstat: Rev. James M. Cafone, S.T.D., *Censor Librorum*
Imprimatur: Most Rev. Theodore E. McCarrick, D.D., Archbishop of Newark

Copyright © 1994 by the International Office of Renew, Archdiocese of Newark, New Jersey

All rights reserved. No part of this book may be reproduced or transmitted in any form or by any means, electronic or mechanical, including photocopying, recording or by any information storage and retrieval system without permission in writing from the Publisher.

Library of Congress Cataloging-in-Publication Data

O'Brien, John E., 1921-
    Refreshed by the word  :  cycle C / by John E. O'Brien.
        p.   cm.
    ISBN 0-8091-3506-X (paper)
    1. Church year meditations.   2. Prayer groups—Catholic Church.
    3. Catholic Church—Customs and practices.   4. Common lectionary—Meditations.
    I. Title
BX2170.C55032                                                                 1994
263′.9—dc20                                                                    CIP

Published by Paulist Press
997 Macarthur Blvd.
Mahwah, N.J. 07430

Printed and bound in the United States of America

# *Contents*

# *Contents*

# Contents

# Acknowledgments

*Refreshed by the Word* is a communal work. I wish to acknowledge and thank the following people who are part of its history.

Msgr. Tom Kleissler, who invited me to write my reflections on the Sunday readings as an instrument for small group faith sharing, and whose critical insights and experiences have helped to sharpen their focus.

Mary C. McGuinness, O.P., for her untiring support and affirmation all through her editing; Rev. John Russell for his helpful theological review and insights.

International Office of RENEW staff members and volunteers for creatively expressing prayers to be used to open the sessions.

Sr. Joan Marie Ricca, S.S.J. and Eileen Brown, for their help in verifying the scripture quotations throughout this work.

Julie Jones, for her typing and research help in preparing the manuscript.

Small Christian community members from the Archdioceses of Newark and Hartford, who piloted various sections and offered valuable comments.

Maria Maggi, editor at Paulist Press, for her encouragement and suggestions.

To all who helped in any way to bring *Refreshed by the Word* to full life I am deeply grateful.

*Dedicated to Betty O'Brien and Bridie Watson
for continued encouragement and support*

# *Foreword*

Father John O'Brien has made a real contribution with this book. Often we rush to the latest, most innovative program for adult religious education. The fact is the church's real textbook is the Bible, specifically the three cycles of the lectionary. How rich the liturgy of the word would become, if folks encountered the word either before or after it is proclaimed in church liturgically. Father O'Brien's materials can be used in a variety of ways—by those in intentional small communities, or by any parish group or ministering group seeking to gain a more communal foundation for their activity. The book could also be used by families. Thus, the book makes possible an experience of church not encountered frequently enough by many Catholics: not only the large assembly, but also church as small group or community, and the domestic church of family.

In Father O'Brien's simple materials, we have the essence of small group experience as well as androgogy at its best: people gathered around God's word, in prayer, sharing their lives with each other, and moving out in action to transform the world.

This book will be of great assistance to groups and communities in the post-RENEW era, as well as for those ministerial, seasonal and small Christian communities who are already making an impact on the church of the future. It is a welcome addition to our collection of pastoral tools.

> *Patrick J. Brennan*
> President, National Center
> for Evangelization and
> Parish Renewal

# *Introduction*

---

A new energy in parish life is emerging throughout the world. Small communities and faith sharing are becoming a more normative part of the very fabric of parish life. This is occurring in a variety of ways. People are gathering in small groups during different seasons of the year to pray, share faith and support one another; people in similar ministries are praying together and sharing faith during their meeting times, thus supporting one another both in their lives and in their ministries; and significant numbers of people are making a commitment to pray and share with others in small communities in an ongoing way, allowing the gospel to touch every aspect of their lives.

*Refreshed by the Word, Cycle C* offers refreshing, lively insights into the word of God. Using the Sunday lectionary readings of Cycle C as a starting point, prayers, reflections, and provocative faith questions are proposed that are applicable to every parishioner, every Christian who desires to grow in the life of God. (Note that the presentation of materials follows the same sequence as the Sunday readings of the lectionary.)

*Refreshed by the Word, Cycle C* can be utilized in a variety of ways. First, the members of parish committees, organizations, and ministries can enhance their time as they gather for their regular meetings. For example, when parishioners on a parish pastoral council or finance council meet, they could use these materials to pray and reflect together and better internalize the values of Jesus in their ministry. Using these materials on a regular basis would insure that all parish meetings become more spiritually based. Instead of lengthening meetings these materials would provide a spiritual enrichment which could focus meetings, help decisions to be made more readily and, in fact, may even shorten many long drawn-out meetings.

1

Second, the materials are also designed in such a way that they can be used by seasonal small groups who gather to share their life and faith at various times during the year. Many parishioners like the concept of meeting seasonally, for example, during Lent and during the autumn. The materials are designed so that people can enter into the process of prayer and faith sharing at any time of the year and be comfortable with the word and the process. And because parishes always have some new parishioners who have not had the experience of being in a small Christian community, inviting parishioners to be part of a seasonal small group gives them a taste of what a small Christian community is about.

Third, the materials offer ample information for parishioners who are entering into or are already involved in small Christian communities. They can be used whether people meet weekly, every other week, or monthly.

## PROCESS

Each group using *Refreshed by the Word* needs to have a small group/community leader or facilitator who is familiar with both the materials and the process. In addition, the leader should check the Ordo or church calendar to ensure that the proper Sunday readings are used. Because the time of Lent and Easter is movable, the Sundays in Ordinary Time are not static either and it would be well for the leader to check the Ordo.

The materials are designed in such a way that the process could take as long as an hour and one half or be as short as twenty minutes. If a seasonal small group or a small Christian community is meeting primarily for prayer and faith sharing, they would use all the components; if a committee or ministerial community is meeting, the participants may wish to read only one or two readings, the reflection, and share briefly on one or two of the sharing questions. If two are selected, the first and third would be most appropriate since they are connected by the same theme.

In order to assist the leader, a missal or missalette which includes the alternative opening prayer for Sunday and the responsorial psalm would be helpful. These can be procured in a number of ways. If the parish has a subscription service, they can order extra copies for small group use or leaders can borrow from the church supply. Often individuals subscribe to a service themselves and can share their copies for the time of meeting.

Leaders are also encouraged to be creative in preparing an appropriate setting for prayer and sharing and to eliminate as far as possible any distractions.

## *Weekly Outline*

### OPENING PRAYER

Each session may begin with a time of focusing on the presence of God through quiet reflection or soft music. The leader may use the alternate opening prayer of the Sunday liturgy, prepare another brief prayer, invite another participant to pray, or choose an appropriate prayer from the Prayer Resources.

### GREETINGS AND ACTION RESPONSE SHARING

At the first session, or whenever there is a new participant, all are invited to introduce themselves and, perhaps, share something about themselves.

At other sessions, this time is used to share with others about experiences that resulted from the previous week's Action Response segment.

### LISTENING AND SHARING THE WORD

Each person reads the scripture silently.

Ideally each participant will have already reflected on the background and the scripture prior to the session. However, it may be helpful to read the background again aloud, followed by a few moments of silence.

Follow with a short prayer invoking the Holy Spirit.

The scripture is then proclaimed aloud, followed by a suitable time of silent prayer.

Each person then shares his/her response to the scripture. The

4 Refreshed by the Word

questions may provide a good guide. The focus is on how one experiences the action of God in his/her life and what that means in daily life.

## ACTION RESPONSE

The leader will help the group focus on specific action responses that could flow from the week's sharing. Each person could choose an individual action, or the group as a whole could choose a common action to undertake. (Suggested Action Responses are included in a separate listing after the Prayer Resource section.) Ministerial communities may simply decide that their tasks at hand will be their response. However, the task at hand need not necessarily be their only response. The word of God always challenges us anew. It is helpful to invite participants to share their commitments. At the beginning of the next session the leader would open with prayer and then invite people to volunteer to share how they carried out their action responses. In this way a gentle form of accountability is used to help people concretely realize how they are living out the word, how they are being "good news" for others.

## PRAYER

The gathering is concluded with some time for prayer. The leader may wish to ask someone to be responsible for leading the closing prayer. Suggested closing prayers are given; however, the leader or participants may wish to select their own or close with spontaneous prayer.

## REMINDER

Any announcements can be made in preparation for the upcoming week or season.

## SMALL GROUP/COMMUNITY FAITH SHARING

Small group/community sessions are a very important part of the parish's spiritual growth and development process. These small groupings provide a rare opportunity for us, the people of God, to share our faith, to listen more closely to the Spirit, and to witness that God has called us, touched us and healed us as individuals, families, neighbors and parishioners.

Understanding and respecting the ways adults learn is an essential part of small faith sharing groups. It is important that the atmosphere be comfortable, warm and friendly. Ambiguity and difference of opinion need to be expected. Each person is given the opportunity to express feelings and thoughts, examined in light of the rich scriptural tradition of our faith. Being accepted and listened to are essential ingredients of a good faith sharing experience. There should be a true desire to listen to another's experience. A sense of humor is always helpful!

The leader/facilitator is the person who has responsibility for guiding the group through the faith sharing and prayers (or assigning it to one of the members) of the small group session. Leaders of the small groups must be well trained for the task. By demonstrating charity and flexibility, a facilitator can effectively help the group to stay on the topic, gently include hesitant members and develop a warm, accepting, open climate and group cohesiveness.

Leaders do not provide preambles or prologues to questions; they do not frighten, shame or argue with participants by word, gesture, expression, voice tone or note taking. Participants may have questions about specific elements of our faith. Rather than trying to answer all questions, the facilitator may refer to the questions beyond the group resources to gain answers about our faith.

A leader listens carefully to the participants and asks questions only when necessary to keep the discussion moving or keep it on focus. The leader needs to be prepared by understanding beforehand the "questions" and the "background" provided in the text. However, the leader need never be a slave to a set of questions or text, but should be able to adapt to what is needed for the sharing as it moves along.

When two or more Christians share our faith, we are assured that Christ is in our midst and that the life of God and gifts of the Spirit are at work in us. Through the small group/community sessions we are in a very vital way opening ourselves to the Spirit's working in us and through us.

## *Faith Sharing Principles*

In an effort to keep your group/community consistent with its purpose, we offer the following Faith Sharing Principles:

## THEOLOGICAL PRINCIPLES

- EACH PERSON IS LED BY GOD ON HIS/HER PERSONAL SPIRITUAL JOURNEY. THIS HAPPENS IN THE CONTEXT OF THE CHURCH.

- FAITH SHARING REFERS TO SHARED REFLECTIONS ON THE ACTION OF GOD IN ONE'S LIFE EXPERIENCE as related to scripture and the church's faith. Faith sharing is not necessarily discussion, problem solving, or scripture study. The purpose is an encounter between a person in the concrete circumstances of one's life and the word of God which leads to a conversion of heart.

- FAITH SHARING IS MEANT TO SERVE OUR UNION WITH CHRIST AND HIS CHURCH AND THEREBY WITH ONE ANOTHER. With the help of God's Spirit we contribute vitality to the whole church. From the church we receive authoritative guidance from episcopal and priestly leadership. We are nurtured in the sacramental life. We are supported with a community of believers for our mission in the world.

- THE ENTIRE FAITH SHARING PROCESS IS SEEN AS PRAYER, i.e., listening to the word of God as broken open by others' experience.

## SMALL GROUP GUIDELINES:

- CONSTANT ATTENTION TO RESPECT, HONESTY AND OPENNESS FOR EACH PERSON WILL ASSIST THE GROUP OR COMMUNITY'S GROWTH.

- EACH PERSON SHARES ON THE LEVEL WHERE HE/SHE FEELS COMFORTABLE.

- SILENCE IS A VITAL PART OF THE TOTAL PROCESS OF FAITH SHARING. Participants are given time to reflect before any sharing begins, and a period of comfortable silence might occur between individual sharings.

- PERSONS ARE ENCOURAGED TO WAIT TO SHARE A SECOND TIME UNTIL OTHERS HAVE CONTRIBUTED WHO WISH TO DO SO.

- THE ENTIRE GROUP IS RESPONSIBLE FOR PARTICIPATING AND FAITH SHARING.

- CONFIDENTIALITY IS ESSENTIAL, ALLOWING EACH PERSON TO SHARE HONESTLY.

- REACHING BEYOND THE GROUP IN ACTION AND RESPONSE IS ESSENTIAL FOR THE GROWTH OF INDIVIDUALS, THE GROUPS AND THE CHURCH.

# *ADVENT SEASON*

# First Sunday of Advent

## OPENING PRAYER

The Alternative Opening Prayer of Today's Liturgy

**READINGS:**     Jeremiah 33:14–16; 1 Thessalonians 3:12—4:2;
Luke 21:25–28, 34–36.

## REFLECTION

The first Sunday of Advent reminds me of two important "signs": first, the end of my time and, second, the hope that God brings. The time of my end is uncertain but the hope based on the Lord's coming is assured.

First, as I reflect on the end of my time, I find myself being touched personally by those contemporaries and those younger than I who die of cancer and heart failure. I spend more time now in reading the obituary page. I am sensitive to people who tell me that I "look good" and then have to add with emphasis "for your age." I know the end of my time is ahead, but I foolishly feel it's a long way off. I distract myself and fail to hear the clear diagnosis of my illness, my spirit becomes bloated with indulgence and worldly cares.

But Advent also balances my predicament with the certain hope that the Lord's coming brings. God tells me that I need not fear the end of time or the end of my time. "Stand erect and raise your heads because your redemption is at hand." And again, "Pray that you have the strength to escape the tribulations that are imminent and to stand before the Son of Man." Advent is a time for listening to the diagnosis of my spiritual illness and to believe the hope that rests in the God who comes to heal.

## SHARING

What are some "signs" of my own end time?

In what way does the phrase "my spirit becomes bloated" refer to my life right now?

How well am I using my remaining time in service to others?

What are some "signs of hope" in my life that God comes in many ways?

How will I be specifically a sign of hope to another this week?

## ACTION RESPONSE

Choose an action that will enable individuals or the group as a whole to live out in the coming week what has been shared.

## PRAYER

Allow time for spontaneous prayer and close with reading aloud the responsorial psalm of Sunday's liturgy, Psalm 25.

# *Second Sunday of Advent*

## OPENING PRAYER

The Alternative Opening Prayer of Today's Liturgy

**READINGS:**    Baruch 5:1–9; Philippians 1:4–6, 8–11;
Luke 3:1–6.

## REFLECTION

Luke reminds us that God's word is always proclaimed in the context of history. The time had come and Luke names all the rulers of the biblical lands who were in power when "the word of God came to John." John fulfills in his own history the prophecies of Isaiah and Baruch and applies the Isaian prophecy to himself.

I am called in the Advent season to hear and fulfill the word of God in my own history. I listen to God's word for years on end and then one day I notice that God's word can seize my attention in a new way. Could this be the season and moment when at last God's word takes root in my heart?

The challenging word is found in Paul's prayer for the Philippians and us. Paul's prayer is "that your love may increase ever more and more in knowledge and every kind of perception: to discern what is of value." What and who really is of value in my life? Where do I give the priorities of time, presence and love?

Is my history calling me to repent and make ready the way of the Lord? Could this Advent be the fullness of time for me to hear at last the word of conversion?

## SHARING

Is there any word that has become alive in me in the last year through sharing and community? What is it?

What is some specific hill that must be leveled or valley that must be filled in my spiritual journey?

Our opening prayer asks that "darkness not blind us to the vision of wisdom." Is there some darkness that we should address? What are those areas of darkness?

How have I adjusted some of my priorities of time this year for "the things that really matter"?

As I reflect on the need for priorities for this coming week, what will those priorities be?

## ACTION RESPONSE

Choose an action that will enable individuals or the group as a whole to live out in the coming week what has been shared.

## PRAYER

Allow time for spontaneous prayer and conclude with reading aloud the responsorial psalm of Sunday's liturgy, Psalm 126.

# Third Sunday of Advent

## OPENING PRAYER

The Alternative Opening Prayer of Today's Liturgy

**READINGS:**  Zephaniah 3:14–18a; Philippians 4:4–7;
Luke 3:10–18.

## REFLECTION

There is a great sense of joy and hope in all the readings today. Zephaniah pictures God as rejoicing *over me*. Why God even "will sing joyfully because of you as one sings at festivals." Paul is on the same key as he says, "Rejoice in the Lord always. I shall say it again, rejoice!" And why? Because the good news is that we have been forgiven and Jesus comes again to call us to celebrate our freedom. We are called to an Advent dance and asked to join the celebration and cry out with joy and gladness. This Advent of Christ is almost too good to be true, so we join the crowd coming out to John and ask, "What then should we do?" As a powerful prophet coming out of the desert, John is also preeminently practical. He tells us to share our clothes and food and to be just in our different occupations whether we are tax collectors or soldiers. The joy of the first two readings and the practical advice of John are not contradictory, "for God loves a cheerful giver" (2 Cor 9:7). Our gift of joy must be shared in our service to others.

The Advent Season is not a little Lent. It highlights the fact that we are sinners, but we are loved sinners who are healed. "I shall say it again, rejoice!" Advent is an invitation to accept a gift of love in

15

Christ. God sings joyfully because of you. Let us join the chorus and sing, "Come, All Ye Faithful."

## SHARING

What images or comparisons come to my mind when I hear Zephaniah say that God will sing because of me as at a festival?

When do I experience the moments of peace that Paul speaks of in my life and community?

What do I think John would say to us if we asked, "What then should we do" in our outreach?

When making requests of the Lord do I follow Paul's advice for gaining peace by praying without anxiety and with gratitude? Share insights.

## ACTION RESPONSE

Choose an action that will enable individuals or the group as a whole to live out in the coming week what has been shared.

## PRAYER

Allow time for spontaneous prayer and conclude with reading aloud the responsorial psalm of Sunday's liturgy, Isaiah 12, 2–3, 4, 5–6.

# Fourth Sunday of Advent

---

## OPENING PRAYER

The Alternative Opening Prayer of Today's Liturgy

**READINGS:**     Micah 5:1–4a; Hebrews 10:5–10; Luke 1:39–45.

## REFLECTION

"Mary set out and traveled to the hill country in haste," to help her older cousin Elizabeth who was also with child. John and Jesus had their first meeting in the dialogue between their mothers. There is insight for us as we prepare for the rebirth of Christ. One of the advents of God is found in ministry. Jesus comes and becomes when we minister to him in one another. Before the word was made flesh and dwelt among us, Mary fleshed out the word in service to her cousin, Elizabeth. The older cousin intuited this kind of advent when she said, "How does this happen to me that the mother of my Lord should come to me?" When I come to Jesus in the hungry, naked and homeless, the advent of Jesus happens again.

In the Cloisters museum in New York City hangs a remarkable painting by an anonymous fifteenth-century Dutch artist. It portrays Mary being advent to Elizabeth in the visitation. Each has an arm around the shoulder of the other. The free hand of each is touching the as yet unborn in the other, a marvelous symbol of spiritual generativity. We touch each other and the Lord comes and becomes more both in dialogue and in service. The Word becomes flesh again in the advent of ministry. When we as community respond to others' needs, Mary's Magnificat resonates in us.

## SHARING

How have I experienced the primacy spoken of in Hebrews of "doing God's will beyond sacrifice"?

What have we as a group done during Advent for the poor of our community? What might have been done?

How do I relate to Elizabeth's question beginning with the words, "How does this happen to me?" How have I experienced an advent in Christ in serving or being served this season?

In what specific way will I help the "Word become flesh" this week?

## ACTION RESPONSE

Choose an action that will enable individuals or the group as a whole to live out in the coming week what has been shared.

## PRAYER

Allow time for spontaneous prayer and conclude with reading aloud the responsorial psalm of Sunday's liturgy, Psalm 80.

# CHRISTMAS SEASON

# Sunday in the Octave of Christmas (Holy Family)

**OPENING PRAYER**

The Alternative Opening Prayer of Today's Liturgy

**READINGS:**     Sirach 3:2–6,12–14; Colossians 3:12–17;
                  Luke 2:41–52.

## REFLECTION

We have all been discouraged at times in identifying with the model of the Holy Family because of unrealistic sermons that we have heard or books that we have read. Today's gospel reminds us that holiness of self or family is not a static state but a progressive journey wherein Jesus progressed in wisdom, age and grace. Likewise did Mary and Joseph progress and so too do our families.

It is worth noting that Jesus was not coddled by his parents. He was given freedom and responsibility like other children of his time. He traveled apart from the elders in the children's caravan. It's comforting, too, to know they were upset at losing him. (How would you feel if you lost your own child?)

When Mary and Joseph found him after the third day, they were not as impressed with his intelligence (as his teachers were) as they were overwhelmed with the loss. If you are a parent don't you identify with Mary's words, "Why have you done this to us? Your father and I have been looking for you with great anxiety"? Have we not experienced the answers of our children who, like Jesus, speak words that are enigmatic at best? "They did not understand what he said to them."

Yet, like most of us, Mary and Joseph continued, went home and reflected in patience, and the fruit of patience began to appear. Jesus was obedient to them and progressed steadily. An honest reading of the gospel is good news for parents who can identify and hope with a family who is always in search of holiness and the ongoing journey of darkness and light.

## SHARING

Are we maturing in our group by giving each person space and responsibility in his/her journey? How do we do this?

Do we have Mary's honesty to question the Lord or to question one another in the group? When has this happened?

How are we doing with patiently reflecting on one another's questions and answers?

What is there in our group experience that has helped the Christ among us to progress steadily?

## ACTION RESPONSE

Choose an action that will enable individuals or the group as a whole to live out in the coming week what has been shared.

## PRAYER

Allow time for spontaneous prayer and conclude with reading aloud the responsorial psalm of Sunday's liturgy, Psalm 128.

# Second Sunday after Christmas

---

## OPENING PRAYER

The Alternative Opening Prayer of Today's Liturgy

**READINGS:**    Sirach 24:1–4, 8–12; Ephesians 1:3–6, 15–18; John 1:1–18.

## REFLECTION

Whenever we speak, our words say something about ourselves, but even our best words don't reflect adequately who we are. Jesus is different. He is the perfect word of the Father. "The word was God." And so Jesus says, "Whoever has seen me has seen the Father" (Jn 14:9). Not only does he speak the Father's word, but also he is one with the Father and is that word.

Later, he will tell us that if we wish to be his disciples "we must make his word our home and we will know the truth that will set us free" (Jn 8:31–32). And again, "Whoever loves me will keep my word, and my Father will love him and we will come to him and make our dwelling with him" (Jn 14:23). When the Spirit comes, the Spirit's chief function will be to teach and remind us of the word of Christ.

In John's gospel, Jesus speaks very simple but powerful words. I am the *way*, the *truth*, the *life*, the *resurrection*, the *good shepherd*, the *vine*. In each instance, the word stands by the reality of who Jesus *is*, and so he must *be* my life, my truth, my share of the risen life. I must *be* the branch living with the intimacy of being called by name. In a world where the word has been cheapened and counterfeited, the original and authentic word is Jesus who must speak because he is the Father's word.

## SHARING

To what degree am I a man or a woman of my word? What examples can others in the group use to verify this?

What does wisdom mean to me in my own life?

Does the word still dwell in our group in a special way? Give an example.

Jesus tells us that only those to whom he reveals God, will see God. Is there a facet of this truth in a line from one of the songs of *Les Miserables*, "To love another person is to see the face of God"? What is an example of this in my own life?

## ACTION RESPONSE

Choose an action that will enable individuals or the group as a whole to live out in the coming week what has been shared.

## PRAYER

Allow time for spontaneous prayer and conclude with reading aloud the responsorial psalm of Sunday's liturgy, Psalm 147.

# Sunday after January 6
# (Baptism of the Lord)

## OPENING PRAYER

The Alternative Opening Prayer of Today's Liturgy

**READINGS:**     Isaiah 42:1–4, 6–7; Acts 10:34–38;
                  Luke 3:15–16, 21–22.

## REFLECTION

Reflection since Vatican II has provided various ways of viewing the church. The servant model views the church, the people of God, as a community serving the needs of people and our world. Baptism is the root of that personal call to ministry as a member of the servant church. The opening prayer on the feast of the Lord's baptism says, "May all who share in the son/daughtership of Christ follow in his path of service to others." The prophet Isaiah speaks of the "servant"..."my chosen one, with whom I am pleased." The exact words that are applied to Jesus as servant in the account of his baptism are the same in all the synoptics.

The reading from the Acts of the Apostles stresses that in the original preaching of Peter Jesus was anointed with the Holy Spirit's power and went about doing good works. Today in the renewal of the church, we stress again that baptism is the radical call to service —the service which, according to Jesus, is the only measure of who is first among us. All that we do and become in our life is in response to the original baptismal call of being a servant of Christ. Jesus says, "Where I am, there also will my servant be" (Jn 12:26). We know where Christ is through the vision of reflective prayer. May we take to heart and to our family and to our workplaces the final mission of our Sunday mass, "Go in peace to love and *serve* the Lord."

## SHARING

We read the second sentence of Isaiah beginning with, "I the Lord called." In what way does this apply to us through baptism?

In his account, Luke has Jesus pray after baptism. How is prayer related to service in Christ's life and ours?

Luke uses the word "fire" to describe the Spirit here and in the Pentecostal account. What does the symbol of fire mean to me?

What advantage does the call to service have when I am in a sharing community?

## ACTION RESPONSE

Choose an action that will enable individuals or the group as a whole to live out in the coming week what has been shared.

## PRAYER

Allow time for spontaneous prayer and conclude with reading aloud the responsorial psalm of Sunday's liturgy, Psalm 29.

# *LENTEN SEASON*

# First Sunday of Lent

---

## OPENING PRAYER

The Alternative Opening Prayer of Today's Liturgy

**READINGS:**     Deuteronomy 26:4–10; Romans 10:8–13;
Luke 4:1–13.

## REFLECTION

Lent is a time when we as individuals and as church return to our Jewish roots in the desert journey of the Old Testament. We hear in the first reading from Deuteronomy of the forty years of wandering in the desert and of the Passover feast which commemorates that experience. In the gospel, Jesus as the new Moses, returns to the desert for forty days and counters all of the temptations of the devil—to worship idols of power, security and pride—by the authentic worship of God alone. Near the end of the Lenten cycle we will hear about Jesus instituting the new Passover of the eucharist which will commemorate the new exodus that leads to the cross and ultimately to union with God.

I recently heard a bishop say that "the greatest spiritual contribution made in America is the Twelve-Step program." Addicts who may be compulsive gamblers, eaters, or drinkers begin in the desert. They admit they are powerless over their addictions. The way from the desert to the oasis of serenity is to surrender to God and become an instrument of God's power. It is a wonderful model for our Lenten journey from the desert of our sinfulness to the oasis of God's grace which is a sharing in Jesus' risen life. Let us begin our journey from Ash Wednesday to Easter with courage and fidelity.

## SHARING

Why do I feel the exodus experience speaks particularly to a pilgrim church and to a group like ours?

How have I ever experienced the word in my heart in the sharing with others in the group?

How do I experience the desert in my life now?

What do I hope to practice or do this Lent to get rid of some of the idols in my life?

## ACTION RESPONSE

Choose an action that will enable individuals or the group as a whole to live out in the coming week what has been shared.

## PRAYER

Allow time for spontaneous prayer and conclude with reading aloud the responsorial psalm of Sunday's liturgy, Psalm 91.

# *Second Sunday of Lent*

---

## OPENING PRAYER

The Alternative Opening Prayer of Today's Liturgy

**READINGS:**       Genesis 15:5–12, 17–18; Philippians 3:17—4:1; Luke 9:28b–36.

## REFLECTION

Luke frequently locates the same events narrated by the other synoptics in the setting of prayer. For him the transfiguration is no exception. Jesus is going to the mountain to pray. While he was praying the transfiguration took place. In prayer we put ourselves at the silent disposal of God. It is a fierce thing to enter into the darkness before the light. Abraham experiences a trance and a "deep, terrifying darkness enveloped him." Then fire appears and passes between the sacrificial offerings and God makes a covenant with Abraham.

So, too, on the mountain with Jesus, Peter and the others fall into a deep sleep symbolizing the darkness. They awaken to the light and glory of the transfigured Lord.

I have never experienced clinical depression but I have dealt with people who have been in that awful distress. They feel as if they are cut off from life, without any meaning or hope. Many are tempted to commit suicide. Ultimately what saves them is God; not an abstract God, but the core and presence of a living God mediated through people who are there for them in a quiet supporting fashion. More important than words, there may be a grasp of the hand or an embrace. The passage for the depressed person from the darkness of abandonment to

31

the light of belonging is a real symbol of our Lenten journey from darkness to light.

## SHARING

How do I fare alone and with the group in silent, wordless prayer in being vulnerable to the Lord?

What most reminds me that "our citizenship is in heaven"? What are some insights from my own experience?

What does the word "covenant" mean to me? Where do I find it most operative in my life?

What time will I specifically make for prayer this week?

## ACTION RESPONSE

Choose an action that will enable individuals or the group as a whole to live out in the coming week what has been shared.

## PRAYER

Allow time for spontaneous prayer and conclude with reading aloud the responsorial psalm of Sunday's liturgy, Psalm 27.

# Third Sunday of Lent

## OPENING PRAYER

The Alternative Opening Prayer of Today's Liturgy

**READINGS:**      Exodus 3:1–8a, 13–15;
1 Corinthians 10:1–6, 10–12; Luke 13:1–9.

## REFLECTION

The Exodus reading gives us an abiding insight into the mystery of God. First, there is fire from the burning bush. It will be a symbol of God and divine energy, the pillar of fire that will guide the exodus by night, and the fire of Abraham's sacrifice that will precede God's covenant. In the New Testament Christ will come to cast fire that will be ignited. The same burning of the heart through the word that Jeremiah experienced will be felt by the disciples on the road to Emmaus. When the Spirit comes at Pentecost it will be in the form of tongues of fire.

Second, God calls Moses by name to indicate there is always an intimate call of God to me. Like Moses and all the people of Old and New Testament times, God called me by my name.

Lastly, God reveals the Godself at once as transcendent, mysterious and ineffable, and at the same time immanent, alive and sustaining all life. Like the dialogue of Tevye in *Fiddler on the Roof*, on the one hand God has no name. God transcends all in a simple "I am." But on the other hand, God is alive in history and is concerned with the suffering of people. God does not remain abstract and aloof. "I am" is also the "God of our ancestors, the God of Sarah and Abraham, Rebecca and Isaac and Rachel and Jacob."

A few years ago when Andrew Greeley conducted one of his national surveys, people were asked if they had ever had an experience of God. A vast majority said they did. Wouldn't Lent be a good time to ask ourselves that question and celebrate the answer of our experience?

## SHARING

Have I ever experienced the burning bush in my prayer, word or service of others? When has this happened?

As I reread the first paragraph of the gospel, how do I see it in relation to my own life experience? What does it say to me this Lent?

Has the image of "one more year" to bear fruit been experienced in our group during this past year? How?

## ACTION RESPONSE

Choose an action that will enable individuals or the group as a whole to live out in the coming week what has been shared.

## PRAYER

Allow time for spontaneous prayer and conclude with reading aloud the responsorial psalm of Sunday's liturgy, Psalm 103.

# Fourth Sunday of Lent

---

## OPENING PRAYER

The Alternative Opening Prayer of Today's Liturgy

**READINGS:**    Joshua 5:9a, 10–12; Corinthians 5:17–21;
Luke 15:1–3, 11–32.

## REFLECTION

Luke's story is about a father prodigal in mercy toward his son. It is a classic of all literature and religion and should be read again out loud. The father lets the son go and the son suffers in his poverty a fate worse than poverty as the last thread of being a Jew is unraveled in the feeding of the pigs. "Coming to his senses" is the poverty of the beatitudes. He makes his amends with God and sets out to tell his earthly father.

The father searches the road every day and when, at last, he sees his son, runs out to embrace him. So happy is he that the son is unable to finish his speech. He will be no second-class citizen. He will not come back as a servant, but as a son. Even though he smells of the road and is tainted by the piggery, the father embraces him and the celebration begins.

The other son comes home from the field and is so angry about hearing the bad news of his brother's return that he refuses to join the party. The father comes out to him to remind him "that you are here with me always; and everything I have is yours." The brother cannot get beyond his concept of justice. The kingdom demands the addition of love. For if he loved the father, he would share in his joy that a brother and son who was dead had come back to life.

Perhaps the parable is really about two parts of one son or one person. Each of us has to join the justice rooted in service with the love learned in loss. Sometimes all of us are fearful of issues dealing with justice or love. We need to integrate the two into our one person. Then we can come in from the isolation of the porch and enter into the celebration.

## SHARING

Joshua tells us that when the Lord provides the grain, the manna ceases. Do I sometimes look to God to make a miracle?

To quote St. Paul, how are we ambassadors or "ministers of reconciliation" to each other before we move out to the larger community? When has this happened?

What part of me still sides with the brother who stays home and is too angry to join the party? Why do I sometimes feel this way?

How and with whom will I be "minister of reconciliation" this week?

## ACTION RESPONSE

Choose an action which will enable individuals or the group as a whole to live out in the coming week what has been shared.

## PRAYER

Allow time for spontaneous prayer and conclude with reading aloud the responsorial psalm of Sunday's liturgy, Psalm 34.

# Fifth Sunday of Lent

---

## OPENING PRAYER

The Alternative Opening Prayer of Today's Liturgy

**READINGS:**      Isaiah 43:16–21; Philippians 3:8–14;
                   John 8:1–11.

## REFLECTION

Today's scriptures remind us not to get bogged down in the mire of the past, but to be free to live in the now and to move ahead.

God speaks through Isaiah, "Remember not the events of the past; the things of long ago consider not. See, I am doing something new!... Now in the desert, I make a way."

Paul writes in Philippians, "Forgetting what lies behind but straining forward to what lies ahead, I continue my pursuit toward the goal."

Then, there is John's account of the woman taken in adultery. The accusers want to use the poor woman to embarrass Jesus. She is but a pawn on a chessboard where they feel they hold all the check moves. If Jesus lets her go he insults Moses. If he condemns her his program of forgiveness is compromised. We know how he solves it— by letting the one without sin cast the first stone, and then writing in the sand to let that thought sink in. There are no takers. They slink away until Jesus is alone with the woman caught in her past.

The woman who is "put down" by men is made to stand. Jesus twice bent down and straightened up. Imagine how the standing woman felt as Jesus knelt before her. He stooped to conquer, to conquer her past sins. He broke the cycle of despair. "Nor do I condemn you. Go, [and] from now on do not sin anymore." The story of her fall and rise is the story of hope for me and for you.

## SHARING

How do I now experience the way of Isaiah, the new way that cuts through the desert of my past?

Read again Paul's pattern of suffering and resurrection in Christ. What in my experience has helped me to learn that pattern?

Are we prone as a group to find fault with people in our parish, finding their failures a part of our attention rather than helping them to break the cycle of their past? What are some examples of when this has happened? What can we do to change our attitudes and behavior in this regard?

## ACTION RESPONSE

Choose an action that will enable individuals or the group as a whole to live out in the coming week what has been shared.

## PRAYER

Allow time for spontaneous prayer and then conclude with reading the responsorial psalm of Sunday's liturgy, Psalm 126.

# Passion Sunday (Palm Sunday)

## OPENING PRAYER

The Alternative Opening Prayer of Today's Liturgy

**READINGS:**    Isaiah 50:4–7; Philippians 2:6–11;
Luke 22:14—23:56 or 23:1–49.

## REFLECTION

In one of his recent publications, Regis Duffy, Franciscan theologian, has given us this rich sentence: "When the text of God's word is located in the context of our life experience, epiphany is not far away." All of us bring our life journey and experience to the word of the passion. God has already spoken to us in our journey experience. Now, hopefully, there will be a convergence of that experience with this word today. Some words will intersect with our lives and an illuminated moment will follow.

We depart from our usual style today. We bring our life to be read by the word. Slowly and reflectively read Luke's passion aloud. Don't rush it. When the reading is finished move apart and reflect for fifteen minutes on what illumination or epiphany took place in prayer. Don't over-analyze as much as be open to the movement and clarification of the Holy Spirit. Return and each one in turn share the distillation of the experience and feelings with the group.

## ACTION RESPONSE

Choose an action that will enable individuals or the group as a whole to live out in the coming week what has been shared.

## PRAYER

Allow time for spontaneous prayer and conclude with reading aloud the responsorial psalm of Sunday's liturgy, Psalm 22.

# EASTER SEASON

# *Easter Sunday*

---

## OPENING PRAYER

The Alternative Opening Prayer of Today's Liturgy

## READINGS:
Acts 10:34a, 37–43; 1 Corinthians 5:6–8; or Colossians 3:1–4; John 20:1–9.

## REFLECTION

John's account of the Easter event is filled with helpful hints and symbols for the disciple following Jesus. First, it is a matter of history that Mary Magdalen came to the tomb driven by love, while the male apostles stayed in their houses in a confused and discouraged state. John will write later in his epistle that "there is no fear in love" (1 Jn 4:18). We might add, neither despair nor confusion. Mary lives out love before John writes about it.

There is almost a humorous scene of John and Peter running to the tomb when Mary tells them that the Lord has been taken from the tomb. In time, John outruns Peter and arrives first but waits for Peter out of respect. Peter enters and looks but there is no conclusion. Then John, the one who loves Jesus, enters and "he saw and believed." Again, faith followed love. Perhaps that is why John's gospel closes with the risen Jesus asking Peter three times if he loves him. The risen Jesus is grasped only in faith and the key to that belief is love. Love the Lord and we will know the heart of Easter faith.

## SHARING

Read 1 Corinthians 5. Explain the image of yeast in your own life.

In Acts, Peter preached about the risen Lord out of his own experience of seeing him. But Jesus tells Thomas, "Blessed are those who have not seen and have believed" (Jn 20:29). Why do we believe?

Do we as a group help each other to "see and believe" in the risen Lord? How do we do this?

How will I live out specifically the call of Jesus to be yeast for others this week?

## ACTION RESPONSE

Choose an action that will enable individuals or the group as a whole to live out in the coming week what has been shared.

## PRAYER

Allow time for spontaneous prayer and conclude with reading aloud the responsorial psalm of Sunday's liturgy, Psalm 118, and reciting together the Sequence (prose text) of "To the Paschal Victim" (see Prayer Resources at the end of this book).

# Second Sunday of Easter

---

## OPENING PRAYER

The Alternative Opening Prayer of Today's Liturgy

**READINGS:**     Acts 5:12–16; Revelation 1:9–11a, 12–13, 17–19; John 20:19–31.

## REFLECTION

In today's gospel we are so anxious to move on to the skepticism of Thomas that we skip over the earlier section when Thomas was absent. It describes the disciples praying together behind locked doors out of fear. Jesus appears before them with the greeting of peace. Then John says that Jesus showed them the wounds of his hands and his side and they rejoiced. They moved from fear to joy because the risen Jesus had come to them—in the phrase of Henri Nouwen—as a "wounded healer."

On Friday the disciples fled when they saw the original wounds inflicted and continued to live in fear. Now the sight of the same wounds filled them with joy. The luminous wounds are signs of healing and joy to them. The scars no longer frighten or discourage, but rather become for them an entry point for healing and experiencing the peace of the risen savior.

As the wounded healer, Jesus asks us to join our wounds with his, putting our hands in his, and to be healed by sharing the pain of the cross and the joy of the resurrection. We are healed to heal. We are called to be wounded healers, to share a story of our healing as an

encouraging entry point for others to know the risen Lord when fear
will be transformed into joy-filled love.

## SHARING

The first reading reveals that the apostles with power witnessed
to the resurrection of Jesus by performing "many signs and wonders"
among the people. Do we expect the same power in our community?

What does the word of John's epistle mean to me when he indicates that everyone who believes in Jesus Christ is begotten by God?

How does our group, in our sharing of individual journeys, qualify to be a community of wounded healers?

In what situations of this coming week will I be a wounded healer
for others?

## ACTION RESPONSE

Choose an action that will enable individuals or the group as a
whole to live out in the coming week what has been shared.

## PRAYER

Allow time for spontaneous prayer and then close with reading
aloud the responsorial psalm of the Sunday's liturgy, Psalm 118.

# Third Sunday of Easter

## OPENING PRAYER

The Alternative Opening Prayer of Today's Liturgy

**READINGS:**   Acts 5:27–32, 40b–41; Revelation 5:11–14;
John 21:1–19.

## REFLECTION

The disciples' journey reaches a special plateau in what is termed the "second call." It is a progression coming out of the original call that manifests a deeper love leading to abandoned trust. In the process, Peter again is the model for all disciples.

In John's gospel (Jn 13:36–38) on the night of the last supper, Jesus tells Peter that he is going somewhere and that Peter cannot follow him "now" but will "later." Typically, Peter wants to come "now" and boasts that he will lay down his life for Jesus. The Lord tells him that before the cock crows, Peter will have denied him three times. We know that Peter does precisely that during the trial of Jesus. The cock crows, he remembers and goes out and weeps bitterly—the beginning of the deeper call.

In today's gospel Jesus appears to the apostles. After feeding them he asks Peter three times if he loves him. The new Peter, chastened by his failure, says after the third time, "Lord, you know everything. You know that I love you." Jesus then calls him to an abandonment that will lead to death for the sake of Christ. Peter is ready. An experience of love leads him through the deeper and second call of the abandoned and trusting disciple. Jesus makes the "later" "now" as he simply says, "Follow me." May we all grow into that loving abandonment of the deeper and second call.

## SHARING

The apostles left the Sanhedrin "rejoicing that they had been found worthy to suffer dishonor" for the sake of Christ. When have I had such an experience? Share how this happened.

Revelation again speaks of the cosmic Christ who receives praise from all creatures. How am I conscious of this hymn of the universe?

Can I say to some degree with Peter, "Lord you know everything. You know that I love you"? What is Jesus' response to me when I speak these words?

What will I do this week to show greater reverence and care for Christ's universe?

## ACTION RESPONSE

Choose an action that will enable individuals or the group as a whole to live out in the coming week what has been shared.

## PRAYER

Allow time for spontaneous prayer and then close with reading aloud the responsorial psalm of Sunday's liturgy, Psalm 30.

# Fourth Sunday of Easter

---

## OPENING PRAYER

The Alternative Opening Prayer of Today's Liturgy

**READINGS:**     Acts 13:14, 43–52; Revelation 7:9, 14b–17;
John 10:27–30.

## REFLECTION

The passage from the Acts of the Apostles has the interesting story of one of the ways in which Paul and Barnabas turned more fully to the Gentiles. The Antioch experience was the first major extension of the good news to the Gentile world. But when the apostles went on mission, they first would go to the synagogues to preach the good news to their fellow Jews. Some of them were converted by the word. However, when the majority of Jews saw the large crowds that Paul was attracting, they became jealous and heaped violent abuse on him. So Paul told them that since they rejected the word of God, he would "now turn to the Gentiles," thus fulfilling the prophetic call by Jesus to Paul on the road to Damascus.

"The Gentiles were delighted" but some of the Jews continued to foment a persecution and expelled Paul and Barnabas from their territory. As always, good came of it. They moved on and because of the persecution they turned more fully to the Gentiles. "The disciples were filled with joy and the Holy Spirit." In persecution and what came out of it, Paul and Barnabas fulfilled to the letter what Jesus called the disciples to feel when he told them to rejoice and dance for joy when others persecute them for his name's sake. Have any of us experienced that dance of joy recently or ever? That's how the birthday of our Gentile opening to the kingdom was celebrated.

## SHARING

In what ways have I known the joy of suffering for Christ?

Reread the passage from Revelation and comment on the joy and hope of the book that for some has become only a doomsday book.

Jesus, our good shepherd, says that no one will ever snatch a sheep from his hand. Share what hope and comfort this passage holds for us.

In what situation in this coming week will I dance the dance of joy and share that with others?

## ACTION RESPONSE

Choose an action that will enable individuals or the group as a whole to live out in the coming week what has been shared.

## PRAYER

Allow time for spontaneous prayer and then conclude with the responsorial psalm of Sunday's liturgy, Psalm 100.

# Fifth Sunday of Easter

---

## OPENING PRAYER

The Alternative Opening Prayer of Today's Liturgy

**READINGS:**     Acts 14:21–27; Revelation 21:1–5a;
John 13:31–33a, 34–35.

## REFLECTION

The theme of the readings in today's liturgy is newness. God did not create only once long ago but continues to create anew every day, every season, every age.

In the first reading from Acts, Paul and Barnabas return to Antioch, having travelled full circle from their first mission journey. They bring the congregation together and relate how God has done something new in opening the door of faith to the Gentiles.

Then, in the second reading from Revelation, John sees "a new heaven and a new earth" and "a new Jerusalem coming down out of heaven from God prepared as a bride adorned for her husband. The one who sat on the throne said, 'Behold I make all things new.'"

Finally, in the gospel Jesus, preparing for his passion and death, leaves, in his last legacy to us, something new. "I give you a new commandment: love one another. As I have loved you, so you should also love one another." What makes this love new is the degree of Christ's unconditional love for us by laying down his life for us while we were still sinners. He asks us to have the same kind of new love for each other. In fact, it becomes a hallmark of discipleship. "This is how all

will know you are my disciples, if you have love for one another."
Have we heard this good news?

## SHARING

Like Paul, how do we share our good news with our group in
order to give reassurance and encourage each other to persevere? Give
some concrete examples of how this has happened.

How do we act as the Lord's stewards in "making all things
new" for each member of our small community?

How do we pass the standards of discipleship among ourselves
in the sign of the new love?

In my relationships during this coming week, who needs to be
reassured and encouraged to persevere by me and when will I do this?

## ACTION RESPONSE

Choose an action that will enable individuals or the group as a
whole to live out in the coming week what has been shared.

## PRAYER

Allow time for spontaneous prayer and then conclude with reading the responsorial psalm of Sunday's liturgy, Psalm 145.

# Sixth Sunday of Easter

**OPENING PRAYER**

The Alternative Opening Prayer of Today's Liturgy

**READINGS:**     Acts 15:1–2, 22–29; Revelation 21:10–14, 22–23;
John 14:23–29.

## REFLECTION

The readings from the Acts of the Apostles has another model of action for the church, not only in apostolic times but also in today's world. Paul and Barnabas had begun to see that when the Gentiles came to the church community, baptism and turning to the Holy Spirit was all that was needed for conversion. They did not need to be circumcised. Now some people came from Jerusalem and caused dissension by saying that the gentiles must also be circumcised or they would not be saved.

So, Paul and Barnabas and others went to Jerusalem to discuss this question, and the discussion and decision is sometimes referred to as the "Council of Jerusalem." At any rate, they concluded that no circumcision was necessary and they wrote out an official letter that stated, in part, "The decision of the Holy Spirit and of us, not to place on you any burden beyond" that which is strictly necessary. They were told to avoid only those practices that would be offensive to the Jewish community, such as pagan sacrifices, strangled animals, or illicit sexual unions.

In every age there are those who will not accept the movement of the Holy Spirit from the experience of the church and the councils.

Those who resist the Spirit in the name of an inauthentic and rigid traditionalism usually end up as bitter schismatics. Would that some who oppose our most recent council, Vatican II, read Acts with openness to the Holy Spirit.

## SHARING

Revelation sees no temple or light in the new Jerusalem because God is the temple and the light. How does this have any relevance to our journey today?

In what ways am I conscious of the effect of the divine indwelling in each of the members of our group?

Do we sometimes forget that the function of the Holy Spirit is not only to teach but to remind us of all that Jesus has told us? How will we try to be more mindful of the Holy Spirit's presence with us?

In what specific situation of the coming week do I most need the power of the Holy Spirit to help me?

## ACTION RESPONSE

Choose an action that will enable individuals or the group as a whole to live out in the week what has been shared.

## PRAYER

Allow time for spontaneous prayer and then conclude with reading the responsorial psalm of Sunday's liturgy, Psalm 67.

# Seventh Sunday of Easter

---

## OPENING PRAYER

The Alternative Opening Prayer of Today's Liturgy

**READINGS:**     Acts 7:55–60; Revelation 22:12–14, 16–17, 20; John 17:20–26.

## REFLECTION

It is comforting to know that at the last supper Jesus prayed for each of us in a way that joins the proclaiming of the word to the apostles. And the object of that prayer in chapter 17 is unity. The same oneness that exists between the Father and the Son may be ours. "I pray...that they may all be one...in us." We don't claim that legacy often enough. We can be assured of the Father and Son being with us in word and in ministry.

The very last verse of this last will and testament is the promise that Jesus will continue to reveal the Father to us. Public revelation may have ended but the heart experience of God continues. I can expect that personal experience because Jesus has willed it so. Again, may we lay claim in faith to our legacy.

What Jesus wants chiefly to reveal is "that the love with which you (the Father) loved me may be in them and I in them." To think that the same love that the Father has for Jesus is being prayed for to be in me. And not only that, but Jesus himself wants to live in me and he prays for that desire of his heart. Isn't this what Paul experiences when he writes, "we are as having nothing yet possessing all things" (2 Cor

6:10)? What more could I ever want than the same union of love and life between the Father and the Son existing in me?

## SHARING

Stephen dies filled with the Spirit and forgiveness. How can I make this my prayer for a happy death?

How do I join with the Spirit and the bride and say to the Lord, "Come, Lord Jesus"?

How do we as a group call upon the prayer of Jesus for us so that we act out of the same love, life and union that exists between Father and Son?

How do we lay claim to our legacy?

As I look to this coming week, how will I bring unity where there may be division?

## ACTION RESPONSE

Choose an action that will enable individuals or the group as a whole to live out in the coming week what has been shared.

## PRAYER

Allow time for spontaneous prayer and then conclude with reading the responsorial psalm of Sunday's liturgy, Psalm 97.

# Pentecost Sunday

**OPENING PRAYER**

The Alternative Opening Prayer of Today's Liturgy

**READINGS:**    Acts 2:1–11; 1 Romans 8:8–17; John 20:19–23.

**REFLECTION**

In the Genesis account of creation, the Hebrew word, *ruah*, is used as wind, breath and spirit. The wind as ruah was sent by God across the chaos and order ensued. God forms from the clay with the breath of the divine ruah a human spirit in women and men sharing the spirit of God and made to God's own image and likeness. Throughout the Old Testament, fire is a special sign of God's active presence. The best known is the theophany to Moses in the burning bush.

Pentecost is the new creation and the new coming of the Holy Spirit. Acts celebrates it with the driving wind reminiscent of Genesis and the tongues of fire, the new and burning presence of God. Writing later, John completes the symbols of Genesis. He pictures the risen Jesus gently breathing on the apostles with a new ruah and inspiration and saying, "Receive the Holy Spirit."

All of these renewals of the Genesis creative symbols say something about the Spirit. Sometimes the Spirit comes as a mighty wind and knocks down and levels walls of ignorance to bring a new beginning. Sometimes the Spirit ignites us prophetically with burning, searing, warming and enlightening fire. Sometimes the Spirit breathes gently upon us as Elijah's small breeze and only with the wisdom of prayer is the Spirit discerned.

Come, Holy Spirit, as mighty wind, prophetic fire or gentle breeze, but come and fill the hearts of your faithful and we shall remake the face of the earth.

## SHARING

How have we as a group experienced the fire of God's word or the zeal of a prophetic stance in our community?

In our parish how do we honor the variety yet equality of age, ethnic, racial and sex differences? How about in our small group?

Do we huddle in fear and in safe sharing with one another, or do we occasionally reach out and risk being led by the Spirit? When has this happened?

What walls of ignorance am I being called upon to knock down this week through the power of the Holy Spirit within me?

## ACTION

Choose an action that will enable individuals or the group as a whole to live out in the coming week what has been shared.

## PRAYER

Allow time for spontaneous prayer and then conclude with reading the responsorial psalm of Sunday's liturgy, Psalm 104, and recite together slowly the Sequence (poetic text), "Come Holy Spirit, Come!" (see Prayer Resources at the end of this book).

# *Trinity Sunday*

## OPENING PRAYER

The Alternative Opening Prayer of Today's Liturgy

**READINGS:**     Proverbs 8:22–31; Romans 5:1–5; John 16:12–15.

## REFLECTION

We have all had the experience of rereading a spiritual or literary classic which we first encountered years ago. But now in a second reading we discover new and deeper meanings. The book is illuminated by all the joys and failures of our intervening life journey. Cardinal John Newman would see it as an illustration of moving from notional to real knowledge. This would seem to be the meaning of the gospel passage today. Jesus tells his disciples and us, "I have much more to tell you, but you cannot bear it now.... The Spirit of truth will guide you to all truth." Jesus further explains that this fuller knowledge will be the shared work of the Holy Trinity: "Everything that the Father has is mine," and the Spirit "will take from what is mine and declare it to you."

One of the key doxologies of the liturgy sums up this movement of the Triune God: "Through him, with him, in him in the unity of the Holy Spirit all glory and honor is yours, almighty Father, forever and ever, Amen." We can only hope that this pattern of the Holy Trinity will act as a light to our spiritual journey as disciples of Christ.

## SHARING

Share how some book or article you have read revealed more insight or wisdom than an earlier reading did.

Can we share some insight of the gospel that has come alive for us in recent years?

How have we experienced the mystery of the Trinity in our life?

## ACTION RESPONSE

Choose an action that will enable individuals or the group as a whole to live out in the coming week what has been shared.

## PRAYER

Allow time for spontaneous prayer and conclude with reading the responsorial psalm of Sunday's liturgy, Psalm 8.

# *Corpus Christi*

---

## OPENING PRAYER

The Alternative Opening Prayer of Today's Liturgy

**READINGS:**     Genesis 14:18–20; 1 Corinthians 11:23–26;
Luke 9:11b–17.

## REFLECTION

We may be apt to forget that the oldest portion of the New Testament is not the gospels but the Pauline letters. St. Paul was martyred before the first gospel was written. That is why today's second reading contains the oldest witness to the words of Jesus at the last supper. They are the same words recited by the priest at the consecration of the mass, "This is my body, this is my blood."

The continuity of that tradition has been made even clearer in our day. The church now gives us the option of taking the eucharist in our hands and feeding ourselves and of drinking from the cup ourselves. Babies are fed. Adults feed themselves. We are called to a new responsibility in taking the eucharist in our own hands.

We should be proud of our Catholic tradition of using the words and becoming part of the sacramental rite. The minister holds the host before us and says, "The Body of Christ." We answer with the original Aramaic word, "Amen." Paul reminds the Corinthians and us in the present tense, "Every time you eat the bread and drink the cup, you proclaim the death of the Lord until he comes."

## SHARING

What does my response with the Aramaic word, "Amen" mean to me?

What implications can we see for all ministry by receiving communion in our hands?

Can we make deeper connections between the eucharistic body of Christ, and the body of Christ in people we meet?

## ACTION RESPONSE

Choose an action that will enable individuals or the group as a whole to live out in the coming week what has been shared.

## PRAYER

Allow time for spontaneous prayer and conclude with reading the responsorial psalm of Sunday's liturgy, Psalm 110.

# SEASON OF THE YEAR
# (ORDINARY TIME)

# Second Sunday of the Year

---

## OPENING PRAYER

The Alternative Opening Prayer of Today's Liturgy

**READINGS:**     Isaiah 62:1–5; 1 Corinthians 12:4–11;
John 2:1–12.

## REFLECTION

In the synoptics there are many miracles recorded as witness to the in-breaking of the reign of God begun by Jesus. In John, however, there is no emphasis on miracles as such and no mention of the reign or kingdom. But there are seven signs, longer descriptions of the work performed by Jesus, to help the disciples come to faith in Jesus and through that faith to new life.

Today's gospel recalls the first of these signs at Cana, where water was changed into wine. The young couple ran out of wine at the wedding feast and they must have been embarrassed. Mary was sensitive to their need and gave good advice for any disciple, "Do whatever he tells you." When Jesus saves the situation by the new wine, the steward says, "You have kept the good wine until now."

The whole symbol in John is that Jesus proclaims a new creation and enhances the original creation by a deeper and fuller life. Wine as the first creation is good, but the new and choice wine is deeper, better and fuller. The first sign took place at Cana and his disciples believed in him.

At the end of the twentieth chapter, John will say to me, "Now Jesus did many other signs...that are not written in this book. But these

are written that you may [come to] believe that Jesus is the Messiah...
and that through this belief you may have life in his name." The sign of
a new life at Cana is not just for the first disciples but for the disciples
of today, you and me.

## SHARING

"As a bridegroom rejoices in his bride, so shall your God rejoice
in you" (Isaiah). What does this mean to me?

While talking about the gifts of the Spirit, Paul uses the phrase
"discernment of spirits." How do we use discernment to name the gifts
of the Holy Spirit in our group?

What are some signs that lead me, as a disciple, to believe that
Jesus is the Christ?

When I reflect on Mary's words, "Do whatever he tells you,"
what is the Lord asking me to do this coming week that will be a sign
of new life for another?

## ACTION RESPONSE

Choose an action that will enable individuals or the group as a
whole to live out in the coming week what has been shared.

## PRAYER

Allow time for spontaneous prayer and close with reading aloud
the responsorial psalm of Sunday's liturgy, Psalm 96.

# *Third Sunday of the Year*

---

## OPENING PRAYER

The Alternative Opening Prayer of Today's Liturgy

**READINGS:**    Nehemiah 8:2–4a, 5–6, 8–10;
1 Corinthians 12:12–30; Luke 1:1–4; 4:14–21.

## REFLECTION

Luke describes Jesus attending the synagogue in Nazareth and searching for a particular text in Isaiah. When he found it he read it as his first proclamation as the expected messiah. He read a passage that had a distinctive messianic overtone. He sat down, which was the normal teaching position of the rabbi, and announced, "Today this scripture passage is fulfilled in your hearing." In this context he was clearly making a messianic claim.

But the word has another and much wider meaning. The whole gospel is at my hand for reading and listening. If I am sincerely praying and seeking the Lord there will be many times that my life experiences will illuminate the word. A passage I may have heard and read a thousand times suddenly comes alive. Like a sword the word pierces my heart and I can hear Jesus saying to me, "Today this scripture passage is fulfilled in your hearing." These are blessed moments in my journey. We recall and treasure them as graced times when Jesus becomes alive and we will never be the same.

## SHARING

Nehemiah says, "Rejoicing in the Lord must be your strength!" Have I forgotten that the gospel means good news? What joyful moments can I recall and share in my faith journey?

We in this group and in our parish are "the body of Christ." How do we honor Christ in each member?

Share a time when a passage from scripture was finally heard by me at heart level, i.e., in a way that moved me to a decision and to a response.

How will I share with others this week the joy of hearing the Lord's words to me as a reflection on the scriptures?

## ACTION RESPONSE

Choose an action that will enable individuals or the group as a whole to live out in the coming week what has been shared.

## PRAYER

Allow time for spontaneous prayer and close with reading aloud the responsorial psalm of Sunday's liturgy, Psalm 19.

# Fourth Sunday of the Year

## OPENING PRAYER

The Alternative Opening Prayer of Today's Liturgy

**READINGS:** Jeremiah 1:4–5, 17–19;
1 Corinthians 12:31—13:13; Luke 4:21–30.

## REFLECTION

Jesus' discussion in the synagogue was well received, but they were looking for miracles, the kind that were reported as having been done in Capernaum. He responded by reminding them that a prophet is not received in his own native place. He then continued and told them that the prophets Elijah and Elisha healed, not Israelites, but people who were gentiles. At these words they grew indignant and wanted to throw him from the hill. At that moment, Jesus exercised a new kind of authority. "He passed through the midst of them and went away."

Like them, we admire and coo over some of the beautiful sections of the gospel and parables and words of mercy and love. But, we too, reject some tough words like those on poverty, abandonment or justice.

Rather than fight or argue over some of the tough passages, we choose sometimes not to listen or, having listened, we refuse to hear. In the geography of my own heart and spirit, I accept the appealing discussions of Jesus, but am guilty at times of outlawing the prophet Jesus in the native place of my heart when he makes demands that would restrict my lifestyle.

## SHARING

Do I truly believe the words spoken by God to Jeremiah, "Before I formed you in the womb I knew you"? Have I ever heard or forgotten this passage? Share times when this has happened.

Read 1 Corinthians 12 again aloud. Then each person make a list of the five most common failures in love and share the list with another.

What will I do this coming week to make right any failures in love that I listed above?

## ACTION RESPONSE

Choose an action that will enable individuals or the group as a whole to live out in the coming week what has been shared.

## PRAYER

Allow time for spontaneous prayer and close with reading aloud the responsorial psalm of Sunday's liturgy, Psalm 71.

# *Fifth Sunday of the Year*

---

## OPENING PRAYER

The Alternative Opening Prayer of Today's Liturgy

**READINGS:**     Isaiah 6:1–2a, 3–8; 1 Corinthians 15:1–11;
Luke 5:1–11.

## REFLECTION

There is a remarkable similarity in the flow of the passages from Isaiah and Luke. In each of them there is a recognition of the awesome power and holiness of God. Isaiah experiences it in the vision of the Almighty as with the attending chorus of praise and smoke that shook the temple. Peter's experience stems from his knowledge as a fisherman but Jesus' command and successful draft of fishes is just as powerful. In each case there is over and against such power and holiness an awareness of personal sinfulness. Isaiah says, "Woe is me...I am a man of unclean lips." Peter cries out, "Depart from me Lord, for I am a sinful man."

Again, there is a similar healing. To Isaiah, God sends an angel to cleanse his lips with a burning coal when he is told, "See, your sin is purged." Jesus tells Peter, "Do not be afraid. From now on you will be catching people." When God asks the prophet Isaiah whom he should send, Isaiah answers, "Here I am...send me!" So, too, with Peter who when cleansed accepts the Lord's invitation. Peter brought his boat to land, left everything and became his follower.

While the two stories are fresh in your mind, recall the similar pattern of your own journey from the recognition of God, our sinfulness, our cleansing and our response to the call and share your reflections with the group.

## SHARING

When did I become aware of the presence of God to a degree that I could not ignore?

What do I think Paul means when he says, "You are being saved, if you hold fast to the word I preached to you"?

How will I be an agent of God's healing and new life for others in this coming week?

## ACTION RESPONSE

Choose an action that will enable individuals or the group as a whole to live out in the coming week what has been shared.

## PRAYER

Allow time for spontaneous prayer and close with reading aloud the responsorial psalm of Sunday's liturgy, Psalm 138.

# Sixth Sunday of the Year

---

## OPENING PRAYER

The Alternative Opening Prayer of Today's Liturgy

**READINGS:**   Jeremiah 17:5–8; 1 Corinthians 15:12, 16–20;
Luke 6:17, 20–26.

## REFLECTION

Our western culture appears secure and confident when it is scientific and logical. It wants definite answers and rewards those who come up with the best answers in the academic, scientific, sport, and business worlds.

The Sermon on the Mount comes as a shocking jolt to the values and reward system of our society. It names "the poor souls and the losers" as blessed, and the rich and the powerful are called to task.

It speaks out of the wisdom of the Middle East and out of probing, prophetic questions that have no simple answers. The poor can surrender eventually to the riches of the kingdom. The hungry shall be fed with the knowledge of the love of God. The weeping will learn what to hope for, and those who are persecuted for Christ's sake should rejoice in anticipation of their reward.

Not so the rich, the well fed, those who laugh at life, the well thought of. To them Jesus says woe, your consolation is now. You shall go hungry, you shall weep, you shall join the false prophets.

We don't understand the beatitudes. We grow into them by long and hard reflection on our life and on our values in relation to Christ.

Then comes the gradual shift born out of poverty when we move from woe to blessed.

## SHARING

How can I illustrate from my own experience the growth of my trust in God compared to the tree planted near the waters?

How do I understand Paul's words, "If for this life only we have hoped in Christ, we are the most pitiable people of all"?

Try the "woe" passages on for size. Let's see how each of us sees them.

In this coming week, how will I try to be more conscious of the challenge of the beatitudes?

## ACTION RESPONSE

Choose an action that will enable individuals or the group as a whole to live out in the coming week what has been shared.

## PRAYER

Allow time for spontaneous prayer and close with reading aloud the responsorial psalm of Sunday's liturgy, Psalm 1.

# Seventh Sunday of the Year

**OPENING PRAYER**

The Alternative Opening Prayer of Today's Liturgy

**READINGS:**    1 Samuel 26:2, 7–9, 12–13, 22–23;
1 Corinthians 15:45–49; Luke 6:27–38.

**REFLECTION**

We hear today the radical call of the gospel. It is relatively easy to love those who love us or to love nice and lovable people. But Jesus says we deserve no credit for this easy or limited love. Sinners do as much. "Even sinners love those who love them."

All love is a gift from God. We don't make love so much as carry it to another or respond to it. When people are lovable it is easy to exercise love and in the process we think we have done the loving. But when it is an enemy or an unlovable one then we know we can't love of ourselves, but we can be the bearer and let God love through us. This is what St. Francis means when he says, "Lord, make me an instrument of your love and forgiveness." We are a human instrument, but still an instrument.

But having a fairly reasonable explanation doesn't make it any easier to love the difficult people. It still demands risks, and at times, looking foolish. So Jesus says we must love with compassion and believe that we are giving when there is no recompense. God is the measure and the norm, not us. And then comes the hope of a "now" reward. If we risk and are instruments, and act out of trust as our Lord asks us, then something will happen. "Give and gifts will be given to

75

you." The measure you measure with will be measured back to you. We act as instruments and we act in faith.

## SHARING

Is David's act too impractical for modern armed camps? Reflect and share.

What does the prayer of St. Francis (see Prayer Resources) say to me about the gospel?

Reread the last paragraph of the gospel beginning with, "Be merciful...."How have I experienced any of the gospel promises in my life?

Who is a person(s) in my daily life whom I have difficulty loving? How will I try to be an instrument of God's love with this person(s) this week?

## ACTION RESPONSE

Choose an action that will enable individuals or the group as a whole to live out in the coming week what has been shared.

## PRAYER

Allow time for spontaneous prayer and close with reading aloud the responsorial psalm of Sunday's liturgy, Psalm 103.

# Eighth Sunday of the Year

## OPENING PRAYER

The Alternative Opening Prayer of Today's Liturgy

**READINGS:**    Sirach 27:4–7; 1 Corinthians 15:54–58;
Luke 6:39–45.

## REFLECTION

We are all guilty in varying degrees of what is called projection. Whenever I judge people by my own prejudices or condemn them for a small share of what I am blind to in myself, I am guilty of projection. It shows up in my being suspicious or judgmental. Jesus puts it this way. "Why do you notice the splinter in your neighbor's eye but do not perceive the wooden beam in your own?" "You hypocrite! Remove the wooden beam from your own eye first; then you will see clearly to remove the splinter in your neighbor's eye."

Who are the scapegoats in my life? Maybe excessive condemnation of what bothers me in myself. Often enough, it is insecurity about one's own sexual orientation which leads to hatred of homosexuals. My own prejudices lead to condemnation of people from other cultures, ethnic groups, races and religions, teenagers, or people with long hair, to name but a few.

The real test of my own inner values and integrity are the fruits that I show forth consistently. "By their fruits you shall know them." And the fruits of the Holy Spirit are a wonderful way of telling about ourselves and others. When clusters of the fruits of the Spirit appear, like love, peace, patience and joy, our hearts and minds are in good shape. Rather than wasting time in looking at splinters in others' eyes, look for the fruits of the Holy Spirit in others' lives and in mine.

## SHARING

Are we people "of our word" or "all talk" or a bit of both? Reflect and share with one another.

Am I convinced of Christ's victory over death for me?

How do we affirm the fruits of the Spirit as they manifest themselves in the members of our group?

What will I do this week to concretely show forth the fruits of the Holy Spirit within me?

## ACTION RESPONSE

Choose an action that will enable individuals or the group as a whole to live out in the coming week what has been shared.

## PRAYER

Allow time for spontaneous prayer and close with reading aloud the responsorial psalm of Sunday's liturgy, Psalm 92.

# Ninth Sunday of the Year

## OPENING PRAYER

The Alternative Opening Prayer of Today's Liturgy

**READINGS:** 1 Kings 8:41–43; Galatians 1:1–2, 6–10; Luke 7:1–10.

## REFLECTION

There is a common thread woven between the readings of Kings and Luke. In Kings, Solomon prays to God to listen to the prayer of a foreigner who is not an Israelite. It actually tells us more about the openness of Solomon than it does about our God who hears all prayers. But the tolerance of Solomon reflected the famous wisdom of his heart.

In Luke there is a description of a Roman centurion asking for a cure for his servant. He uses his military background of telling a man to come and he comes, to go and he goes, to explain that Jesus doesn't have to enter his house to effect the cure. Christ, like the centurion on another level, can order the illness to go and it goes. Jesus is deeply touched by this man and not only does he heal the sick servant but he says, "I tell you, not even in Israel have I found such faith."

How fitting that from the earliest of times until now the centurion's words are placed on the lips of Christians when they come to the eucharist. "Lord, I am not worthy to receive you but only say the word and I shall be healed." How paradoxical that at the most sacred of times the words of a communicant come not from a Christian or a Jew but from a pagan Roman soldier.

## SHARING

In our shifting parishes, perhaps our own, we sometimes resent strangers and foreigners coming to our church on Sunday. How have we tried to be welcoming of others?

How might there be tension in me and the group about the difference between "a different gospel" and authentic growth and renewal?

When have I found wisdom, encouragement or hope in the words of a stranger?

What are some of the healing words that have been said in our Sunday liturgy?

In what specific ways this week will I offer authentic hospitality to another?

## ACTION RESPONSE

Choose an action that will enable individuals or the group as a whole to live out in the coming week what has been shared.

## PRAYER

Allow time for spontaneous prayer and close with reading aloud the responsorial psalm of Sunday's liturgy, Psalm 117.

# *Tenth Sunday of the Year*

---

## OPENING PRAYER

The Alternative Opening Prayer of Today's Liturgy

**READINGS:**     1 Kings 17:17–24; Galatians 1:11–19;
                  Luke 7:11–17.

## REFLECTION

The parallel between the first reading about Elijah and the description in Luke about Jesus is very evident. Both revolve around a widow's son who dies. In each instance, Elijah and Jesus restore the dead one to life, and in each situation the conclusion is that a great prophet had arisen among the people and his word was honored.

It is also possible that in the Lukan account Jesus has a premonition of what "sort of sorrow" would pierce his own mother's heart when he would be seized and ultimately put to death before her eyes. Did Jesus perhaps see his own mother in the widow of Naim and do for her what he would not do for his own mother? Only the trust in his own Father resurrected Jesus at Easter. There is no record in the gospels of his meeting his mother. This is probably because it is so personal. As in the case of his relationship with his Father in prayer only those involved were privy to it. But it is safe to presume that after Easter, he appeared to Mary and what he did at Naim he did then through the Father. "Jesus gave him to his mother." John's comment applies here. "There were many other things that Jesus did but they are not recorded in this book." Some things were just too personal.

## SHARING

When have I applied to God the accusation of the mother against Elijah, "Why have you done this to me?"

What do I say or do when I visit parents who have lost a child?

When did God give back to you something or someone who was very dear to you? Share what that meant to you?

How will I specifically be a source of comfort to another this week?

## ACTION RESPONSE

Choose an action that will enable individuals or the group as a whole to live out in the coming week what has been shared.

## PRAYER

Allow time for spontaneous prayer and close with reading aloud the responsorial psalm of Sunday's liturgy, Psalm 30.

# Eleventh Sunday of the Year

## OPENING PRAYER

The Alternative Opening Prayer of Today's Liturgy

**READINGS:** 2 Samuel 12:7–10,13; Galatians 2:16, 19–21; Luke 7:36—8:3.

## REFLECTION

In the renewal of the sacrament of reconciliation the celebration of the penitent should be one of joy and gratitude for the God who has been forgiving us in our daily journey. We come to the sacrament in order to experience more concretely the forgiveness of God and to be reconciled with the community of the faithful.

That is what the story in Luke signifies. The prodigal son who asked God's forgiveness, had to speak it as well to his earthly father. So, too, the woman at the banquet. For her, celebration is not in words but totally in some symbolic actions. She takes all the tools of her trade and lets them speak in a silent Magnificat. Her eyes, hair, ointment and kissing of the feet of Jesus are used to sing of her love of the Lord who has heard her voice of sorrow for sins.

Her actions toward Jesus are the very things which had been denied him by the lack of hospitality on the part of the host. To put Jesus in his place and to remind him that he came to the banquet not as an equal but as a speaker or entertainer, the ordinary signs were denied him.

Jesus reads the feigned shock and disdain for the "sort of woman...touching him." By the illustration of forgiveness of two debtors, Jesus leads the host to admit that if more is forgiven, then more love is shown. The woman's love was the reason why she came to sing out her silent Magnificat of joy and gratitude for forgiveness.

## SHARING

Our God is a God who goes beyond justice and forgives with a full measure of love. What about me? How am I doing at forgiveness of others?

Paul says that he still has his human life but it is a life of faith in the Son of God. What helps me to say this with the same conviction?

When has a great measure of love been shown to me in forgiveness by another?

In what specific way will I be a reconciling person this week?

## ACTION RESPONSE

Choose an action that will enable individuals or the group as a whole to live out in the coming week what has been shared.

## PRAYER

Allow time for spontaneous prayer and close with reading aloud the responsorial psalm of Sunday's liturgy, Psalm 32.

# Twelfth Sunday of the Year

## OPENING PRAYER

The Alternative Opening Prayer of Today's Liturgy

**READINGS:**    Zechariah 12:10–11; 13:1; Galatians 3:26–29;
Luke 9:18–24.

## REFLECTION

One of the biblical terms that we have barely begun to listen to, and even less appropriate, is the term and reality, "disciple." We often have only vague ideas of some kind of following. In the words of Bonhoeffer, we have cheapened discipleship.

Today's gospel has two of the central conditions for being a disciple. One is a question and one is a challenge. First, we cannot hide with the crowd saying who Jesus is in the words of someone else. We have to hear it clearly, "But who do you say that I am?" Peter answers, "The Messiah of God." Each of us has to face and answer that question in a personal I-Thou relationship with Jesus. Is he for me the Christ, the Messiah? This perennial faith question is the foundation of all discipleship.

Secondly, there is a cost of discipleship. If we are to follow Jesus we must deny our very self, take up our cross each day and follow in his steps. "Whoever loses his life for my sake," Jesus says, "will save it." Jesus took up the cross, and to be his disciple so must I. The cross will be a honing instrument to cleanse and pare away the false me so that the real authentic self will emerge. I must make sure that I answer the question and accept the challenge of the disciple. The question is,

85

"Who do you say that I am?" and the challenge is, "Take up your cross and follow me." If I want to be a disciple, I can at least begin by listening to the question and taking up the challenge.

## SHARING

"My soul is thirsting for you, O Lord, my God" (Responsorial Psalm 63). Read the first two verses, reflect on them and share.

How do we in this group really honor Paul's statement, "There is not male and female; for you are all one in Christ Jesus"? How about in our parish?

In light of my own life experience and prayer, what descriptive answer would I give to Jesus' question, "Who do you say that I am?"

What particular cross of discipleship am I being called to take up this coming week?

## ACTION RESPONSE

Choose an action that will enable individuals or the group as a whole to live out in the coming week what has been shared.

## PRAYER

Allow time for spontaneous prayer and close with reading aloud the responsorial psalm of Sunday's liturgy, Psalm 63.

# Thirteenth Sunday of the Year

## OPENING PRAYER

The Alternative Opening Prayer of Today's Liturgy

**READINGS:** 1 Kings 19:16b, 19–21; Galatians 5:1, 13–18; Luke 9:51–62.

## REFLECTION

Two great truths are articulated in today's gospel. First, we find that the theme of journey is most important for Luke. In his gospel, he has Jesus journeying from Nazareth to Jerusalem where he dies, rises and ascends to the Father with the promise of the Spirit. The second volume, Acts, has the Spirit coming at Pentecost. Then starts the new journey of the community, which Jesus began at Jerusalem, to the pagan world (symbolized by Rome), where the journey comes to an end but does not stop. The journey continues in the life of the church today and in the lives of Jesus' disciples. So the importance of today's phrase in the ninth chapter of Luke, "He resolutely determined to journey to Jerusalem," and the disciples' journey, too, must be based on that same firm resolve.

The second truth is another feature of the cost of discipleship. Some say to Jesus, "I want to follow you," but Jesus reminds them that there is less security in this than there is for the foxes who have their dens and the birds who have their nests. For the disciple, like Jesus, has "nowhere to lay his head." Another wants to follow but first has to bury his father. This is a delaying tactic. Jesus answers, "Let the dead bury their dead." He uses the image from the first reading wherein

87

Elisha is willing to slay his oxen, burn the yoke and give the boiled meat away. So, from this image, Jesus says to his disciples, "No one who sets a hand to the plow and looks to what was left behind is fit for the kingdom of God." Tough truths for the disciples to hear but even tougher to live out. Nothing but nothing can come before the disciples' journey into the kingdom of Jesus.

## SHARING

Do we take the call of discipleship as seriously as Elijah did and demanded of Elisha?

How do we as a group qualify for Paul's statement, "Serve one another through love"?

Which of the three demands of following Jesus in today's gospel do I find the most difficult to live up to?

What will I do this week to respond to the call of discipleship in the area that is most difficult for me?

## ACTION RESPONSE

Choose an action that will enable individuals or the group as a whole to live out in the coming week what has been shared.

## PRAYER

Allow time for spontaneous prayer and close with reading aloud the responsorial psalm of Sunday's liturgy, Psalm 16.

# Fourteenth Sunday of the Year

---

## OPENING PRAYER

The Alternative Opening Prayer of Today's Liturgy

**READINGS:**    Isaiah 66:10–14c; Galatians 6:14–18;
Luke 10:1–12, 17–20.

## REFLECTION

Due to ignorance or a partial reading of a few Old Testament passages, a lot of people think of the God of the New Testament as a God of love, but the God of the Old Testament as one concerned with punishment and justice. God is sometimes caricatured as a "Gottcha" God waiting in hiding and then pouncing upon us with our first mistake.

Nothing can be further from the truth. Overall, the God of the Old Testament is very loving, with a fierce passionate love. God pursues the people like a wild lover and will not give up. Isaiah gives us an inkling of this kind of quality in the God of revelation. Listen to this tenderness. "Rejoice with Jerusalem and be glad because of her, exult, exult with her, all you who were mourning over her. Oh, that you may suck fully of the milk of her comfort, that you may nurse with delight at her abundant breasts!" He goes on then to say that God will carry her people in her arms and fondle them in her lap. Finally, "As a mother comforts her child, so will I comfort you; in Jerusalem you shall find your comfort. When you see this, your heart shall rejoice.... The Lord's power shall be known."

After that wild description who could ever cling to a threatening and punishing God. There's only one difficulty. If we choose Isaiah's picture of God and we are made to God's image and likeness, we may have to change quite a bit ourselves to be that kind of a passionate, loving person responding to our God.

## SHARING

How do you like Isaiah's portrayal of God as a mother?

Paul indicates that all that matters is that one is created anew. Does it really matter to me that I am created anew? In what ways?

What and who really matters in my life?

How are we doing in traveling "light" in our journey of discipleship?

## ACTION RESPONSE

Choose an action that will enable individuals or the group as a whole to live out in the coming week what has been shared.

## PRAYER

Allow time for spontaneous prayer and close with reading aloud the responsorial psalm of Sunday's liturgy, Psalm 66.

# Fifteenth Sunday of the Year

## OPENING PRAYER

The Alternative Opening Prayer of Today's Liturgy

**READINGS:**     Deuteronomy 30:10–14; Colossians 1:15–20;
                  Luke 10:25–37.

## REFLECTION

Lawyers seek precision in the law. Thus, a lawyer asked Jesus in today's reading, "What must I do to inherit eternal life?" Jesus met him on his own ground and asked him what was written in the law. The lawyer answered by quoting the Mosaic triad of love—God, neighbor and self. So Jesus accepted it with the suggestion, "Do this and you will live."

But the lawyer "to justify himself" asked, "And who is my neighbor?" Jesus might have stayed again on the lawyer's own turf and defined what a neighbor was with a reference to legal tradition and precedence and the debate might still be going on. Instead, Jesus moved the argument from head to heart and told a good story. It was the tale of a man who was on the road from Jerusalem to Jericho who was mugged, stripped and left half dead. Then, the respectable people like a priest and Levite passed him by. They did not want to get involved. The most unlikely person, a Samaritan, stopped. (This would be as shocking as a Ku Klux Klan member stopping to attend an African American.)

The Samaritan gave the injured person first aid, took him to an inn, stayed overnight and left a deposit on the bill and said he would return and pay the balance in the morning. Then Jesus said to the lawyer, "Which of these three...was neighbor?" And the lawyer answered that it was he who showed compassion. Jesus then gave the practical conclusion, "Go and do likewise." Next case!

## SHARING

Moses tells us where the command and word of God is, namely, in our heart. Have I discovered God's word and command there? In what ways?

Paul talks about the cosmic Christ. How would I summarize what goes into that title from my experience?

*My Fair Lady* has a song, "Don't Talk of Love, Show Me." How have we gotten past merely talking in our group?

## ACTION RESPONSE

Choose an action that will enable individuals or the group as a whole to live out in the coming week what has been shared.

## PRAYER

Allow time for spontaneous prayer and close with reading aloud the responsorial psalm of Sunday's liturgy, Psalm 69.

# Sixteenth Sunday of the Year

## OPENING PRAYER

The Alternative Opening Prayer of Today's Liturgy

**READINGS:**    Genesis 18:1–10a; Colossians 1:24–28;
Luke 10:38–42.

## REFLECTION

In the gospel of last Sunday, Luke extols the Good Samaritan as one who is truly neighbor and the lawyer was told, "Go and do likewise." There immediately follows a story which calls for the counterbalance of prayer.

Jesus goes to Bethany and eats with Martha and Mary. Martha welcomes him and is busy with the details of hospitality. All the while, her sister Mary sits at the feet of Jesus and listens to his words. Martha grows upset at doing all the work alone in the kitchen. Interestingly, she tells Jesus how he should feel and what he should do. "Lord, do you not care that my sister has left me by myself to do the serving? Tell her to help me."

Jesus ignores her two directives and replies, "Martha, you are anxious and worried about many things. There is need of only one thing. Mary has chosen the better part and it will not be taken from her."

The listening Mary is the balance for the action of the Good Samaritan. (In time Ignatius Loyola would call us to be contemplatives in action.) At a later point in her life Martha is extolled just as the Good Samaritan is (Jn 11). But for now, not only is this story today a balance of prayer and action, Mary and the Good Samaritan, but it is also a story of elevating the role of women. Women are seen and recognized as capable and worthy of spending time in contemplation.

## SHARING

Authentic hospitality should be generative of new life. How have we as a group experienced that connection?

In Colossians, Paul says, "In my flesh I am filling up what is lacking." How does this text challenge me in my own personal life?

Which side of Martha/Mary's union needs more balance in my life?

In what specific ways will I act upon the call to a balance of prayer and action this week?

## ACTION RESPONSE

Choose an action that will enable individuals or the group as a whole to live out in the coming week what has been shared.

## PRAYER

Allow time for spontaneous prayer and close with reading aloud the responsorial psalm of Sunday's liturgy, Psalm 15.

# Seventeenth Sunday of the Year

## OPENING PRAYER

The Alternative Opening Prayer of Today's Liturgy

**READINGS:**    Genesis 18:20–32; Colossians 2:12–14; Luke 11:1–13.

## REFLECTION

Two of the threads that run throughout the gospel of Luke are prayer and the role of the Holy Spirit. Today's gospel illustrates both.

First is the theme of prayer. The other synoptics have Jesus teaching the Our Father as a model of prayer. But Luke alone has it in the context of Jesus' own prayer. One day Jesus was praying. When he had finished the disciples asked, "Lord, teach us to pray" and Jesus gave them the Lord's Prayer. He goes on to tell them to pray with persistence. "Ask and you will receive, seek and you will find, knock and the door will be opened to you." If we ask as Jesus asks, we shall receive many different and more generous gifts than ever we imagined. Seek, yes, but we must allow God to surprise us at what we find under God's direction in the seeking. We cannot direct the program, the time or even the door that will open. God may open it in time or one may open at my side or my back, not necessarily the one I'm looking at.

The second thread is the Holy Spirit. It flows from what was just said that God will surprise us. God has to be infinitely better than a good father. If a son asks for an egg, we do not give him a scorpion, and if we who are so imperfect can give so much, how much more will God give us. The other synoptics say God will give us "good things."

Luke says God will give us "the Holy Spirit." In Luke's vision there is more of a nuance that we, with the Spirit, will choose the good things, developing our responsibility and our power of discernment.

## SHARING

What are our reactions and insights into the reading from Genesis? Why was Abraham able to talk God out of the destruction promised?

What a colorful image from Colossians, that God cancelled the bond against us and "removed it from our midst, nailing it to the cross." How does this image encourage me?

Do we sometimes project an image of an authoritarian father or mother onto God, making God to be a poor image and caricature of ourselves? Share when and how this has happened.

## ACTION RESPONSE

Choose an action that will enable individuals or the group as a whole to live out in the coming week what has been shared.

## PRAYER

Allow time for spontaneous prayer and close with reading aloud the responsorial psalm of Sunday's liturgy, Psalm 138.

# Eighteenth Sunday of the Year

## OPENING PRAYER

The Alternative Opening Prayer of Today's Liturgy

**READINGS:** Ecclesiastes 1:2; 2:21–23;
Colossians 3:1–5, 9–11; Luke 12:13–21.

## REFLECTION

All the scripture readings today hammer away at one theme—
that overconcern with material goods can stifle our life in God.

In the gospel Jesus chides the rich fool who built bigger grain
bins "but is not rich in what matters to God." Today we can fall into a
similar trap of idolizing our mutual funds and stock holdings and missing the spiritual in our lives.

The final scene of the classic movie, *Citizen Kane*, is a good
illustration of the gospel reading. Kane, a multimillionaire, is on his
deathbed in his huge mansion and the only word he keeps repeating is
"Rosebud." The scene shifts to a huge cellar where servants are stoking
a furnace. The next item to feed the fire is a small sled with the image
of a rosebud painted on its boards. It was a symbol of the only happy
moment Kane could recall, when as a small boy he coasted on that
Rosebud sled. Then into the furnace it goes. "Vanity of vanities! All
things are vanity."

To insure our future is a valid concern as long as there is a balance with our spiritual lives; Jesus cautions us that we do "not live by
bread alone" (Lk 4:4). Christian disciples are to be stewards of their
time and apportion a generous share to prayer, scripture reading and

service to others. There is less chance that our material goods will become our idols if we share enough with the poor so as to keep our hearts focused on "what is above."

## SHARING

What are some practical ways we manifest our priority of seeking "what is above"?

Is there any word of the gospel that you sometimes "harden your heart" against?

How do you experience Paul's words, "Your life is hidden with Christ in God"?

Have we as a small community shared our goods this year with the poor in our town?

## ACTION RESPONSE

Choose an action that will enable individuals or the group as a whole to live out in the coming week what has been shared.

## PRAYER

Allow time for spontaneous prayer and conclude with praying the responsorial psalm of Sunday's liturgy, Psalm 95.

# Nineteenth Sunday of the Year

## OPENING PRAYER

The Alternative Opening Prayer of Today's Liturgy

**READINGS:**     Wisdom 18:6–9; Hebrews 11:1–2, 8–19;
Luke 12:32–48.

## REFLECTION

We are by nature people who want answers and assurances, while God often calls us to live out the questions and to trust. The readings on this day hammer away at that facet of the experience of faith.

Wisdom tells us that the people of the Passover might "put their *faith*" in the promises of God and "your people *awaited* the salvation of the the just." How foreign to our controlling egos are God's words of "faith" and "await."

Hebrews extols the virtues of Abraham our ancestor in faith. He obeyed and went forth not knowing where the journey was calling him. He trusted and his wife Sarah conceived. He trusted even to sacrifice his son and gained back not one son but many "descendants as numerous as the stars in the sky and as countless as the sands on the seashore."

Luke's gospel has the disciples of the master being "ready," "awaiting the Master's return," "opening without delay," "wide awake." These qualities must be apparent because the Son of Man will come when you least expect him.

There are times we must exhibit the serpent's wisdom but we

99

must never forget the trust of the simple dove. Today's words are an antidote to our compulsion to be in total control.

## SHARING

Take the first sentence of Hebrews about faith and see what practical examples it evokes in our own lives.

In what ways do I identify with Abraham and Sarah as our ancestors and models of faith?

Am I "wide awake, ready and waiting" for the Lord's presence in my life? How?

In what specific ways will I act on the Lord's call to turn over control to him this week?

## ACTION RESPONSE

Choose an action that will enable individuals or the group as a whole to live out in the coming week what has been shared.

## PRAYER

Allow time for spontaneous prayer and close with reading aloud the responsorial psalm of Sunday's liturgy, Psalm 33.

# Twentieth Sunday of the Year

## OPENING PRAYER

The Alternative Opening Prayer of Today's Liturgy

**READINGS:**     Jeremiah 38:4–6, 8–10; Hebrews 12:1–4;
Luke 12:49–53.

## REFLECTION

One of the subtle ways we can crucify Jesus again is to domesticate him. Let him say only the nice things; keep only those parts of the gospel that are not challenging; keep him so bland in agreeing with all views that he has to spit himself out of our mouths. So it's a good jolt to hear the prophet Jesus speak in the context of the rejection of all prophets.

Jeremiah shows us what the lot of most prophets must be. "He is not interested in the welfare of our people" and so he is maligned publicly because he says the unpopular things. Eventually, to silence him, he is thrown into a cistern and has to wallow in mud.

The author of Hebrews tells us to learn from Jesus what our prophetic stance ought to be. Jesus "endured the cross, despising its shame," and "such opposition from sinners." He tells us the only way we can keep our prophetic eyes strong and our courage up is to persevere and keep "our eyes fixed on Jesus" and not grow despondent or abandon the struggle.

Imagine how popular Jesus' words must have made him when he said, "I have come to set the earth on fire, and how I wish it were already blazing!" He would seem then and now to be out of control to

101

people who want religion to be neat and just legal. Can you imagine how his words stung? "Do you think that I have come to establish peace? No, I tell you, but rather division." Then he specifies how the cost of peace will at times even break up families. Do I take my baptismal anointing as prophet seriously? Do I dare to be ignited with the fire of the prophet Jesus?

## SHARING

Like Jeremiah, when have my words and life led to strong opposition or being excluded?

In the context of a prophetic stance, what does the Hebrews' word, "Keep your eyes fixed on Jesus," mean to me?

What Christ-values threaten peace in my family or parish?

In what specific situations this week am I being called to take a prophetic stand?

## ACTION RESPONSE

Choose an action that will enable individuals or the group as a whole to live out in the coming week what has been shared.

## PRAYER

Allow time for spontaneous prayer and close with reading aloud the responsorial psalm of Sunday's liturgy, Psalm 40.

# Twenty-First Sunday of the Year

## OPENING PRAYER

The Alternative Opening Prayer of Today's Liturgy

**READINGS:**     Isaiah 66:18–21; Hebrews 12:5–7, 11–13;
Luke 13:22–30.

## REFLECTION

Like a great symphony there's frequent counterpoint between
Isaiah and Jesus. Now one, now the other will interplay and illuminate,
and then those glorious moments of harmony. Today's readings illustrate how the prophet sets the early stage for the final moment of Jesus.

Isaiah prophesies that all the nations of the world will be called
by God to come and see the beauty of the Lord in Jerusalem. Even
more remarkable is the prophecy voiced by Isaiah, "Some of these I
will take as priests and Levites, says the Lord."

When Jesus comes as the messiah of Isaiah's hopes, he finds a
people who are very inbred. They have little tolerance for Samaritans or
Syro-Phoenicians and hate the Roman overlords. Jesus speaks the Isaian
theme, "People will come from the east and west and from the north
and south and will recline at table in the kingdom of God. For behold,
some are last who will be first, and some are first who will be last."

There is no "in" group for Jesus. Blood or nationality are not
enough. "Only he or she who hears and keeps my word is my brother
or sister." How is my citizenship in the kingdom and membership in
Christ's family faring?

## SHARING

Demographers tell us that by the year 2000, 80 percent of the church will be in or from the developing countries. How does this prediction meld with Isaiah?

How would I explain from Hebrews the common root of discipline and disciple?

Are we sometimes like some of the Pharisees of Jesus' age, more Catholic than catholic? What are some examples of this?

Are there situations in my life where I can be more inclusive this week? As a small group/community are we inclusive in whom we welcome to share life and faith?

## ACTION RESPONSE

Choose an action that will enable individuals or the group as a whole to live out in the coming week what has been shared.

## PRAYER

Allow time for spontaneous prayer and close with reading aloud the responsorial psalm of Sunday's liturgy, Psalm 117.

# Twenty-Second Sunday of the Year

## OPENING PRAYER

The Alternative Opening Prayer of Today's Liturgy

**READINGS:**     Sirach 3:17–18, 20, 28–29;
                  Hebrews 12:18–19, 22–24a; Luke 14:1, 7–14.

## REFLECTION

When the ancients said, *In medio stat virtus*, they meant that virtue is a balance, not a compromise between extremes. It is hard to keep that balance so Sirach and Jesus addressed the imbalance. They both talked about the virtue of humility which is a balance between the wimp and the bully. Jesus was neither. Only a person who was integrated in that balance could say, "I lay down my life in order to take it up again. No one takes it from me" (Jn 10:17–18).

Jesus is in the tradition of Sirach who says, "The mind of a sage appreciates proverbs." While the Pharisees who invite Jesus to dine observed him closely, he continued with sustained wisdom. Sirach would have enjoyed his statement, "Everyone who exalts himself will be humbled, but the one who humbles himself will be exalted." If people are so obsessed with their rights in an aggressive style they will get their comeuppance eventually. They will be humbled. But if they live within their own gifts and abilities with serenity, others will accept and respect them for their humility and thus will they be exalted.

May we seek the balance of Christ who humbles himself even to the cross and because of this God has exalted him and "given him the name above all other names." It is an application of another bit of

Jesus' wisdom. "Seek first the kingdom and other things will be given to you."

## SHARING

How do I think Sirach would do in a self-help group seeking a better self-image?

On what side of Hebrews' description of the old and new do I find myself, and to what degree?

What do I think Jesus means when he says to invite people to dinner who cannot repay you?

In what specific ways will I act on the call of the Lord for balance in my life?

## ACTION RESPONSE

Choose an action that will enable individuals or the group as a whole to live out in the coming week what has been shared.

## PRAYER

Allow time for spontaneous prayer and close with reading aloud the responsorial psalm of Sunday's liturgy, Psalm 68.

# Twenty-Third Sunday of the Year

**OPENING PRAYER**

The Alternative Opening Prayer of Today's Liturgy

**READINGS:**       Wisdom 9:13–18b; Philemon 9–10, 12–17;
Luke 14:25–33.

## REFLECTION

While he was in a concentration camp, Dietrich Bonhoeffer wrote the book, *The Cost of Discipleship*. In it he criticized what he called "cheap grace." Rather, discipleship is demanding. Today's gospel challenges us with a hard saying that grace cannot be gained without cost of self.

Jesus says that to be a disciple we have to be willing to forsake all things: our possessions, our family, even what we consider to be ourselves. He illustrates it with two descriptions, of a man about to build without the necessary money, or a king about to enter battle without adequate troops. He said each should stop building and battling. We should know clearly what we are getting into, what we are being asked by the situation. So in discipleship, Jesus says we should not follow unless we are aware of the cost involved and have the willingness to do what is demanded.

The paradox is that the disciple who gives up all finds in freedom a new relationship toward family, a freer use of possessions and, above all, the discovery of the true self. The one who loses his life for the kingdom or reign of God will find it. Discipleship is not cheap, but the investment made with generosity will lead to a harvest of a hundredfold.

## SHARING

Do we consistently pray for wisdom to help us in our personal and community problems? When has this happened?

Can we identify with the tenderness of Paul who in sending Onesimus is "sending...my own heart"? In what ways?

What does the demand "Take up your cross and follow me" mean to me as a disciple of Christ?

What cross am I being asked to take up in a specific way this week?

## ACTION RESPONSE

Choose an action that will enable individuals or the group as a whole to live out in the coming week what has been shared.

## PRAYER

Allow time for spontaneous prayer and close with reading aloud the responsorial psalm of Sunday's liturgy, Psalm 90.

# Twenty-Fourth Sunday of the Year

## OPENING PRAYER

The Alternative Opening Prayer of Today's Liturgy

**READINGS:** Exodus 32:7–11, 13–14; 1 Timothy 1:12–17;
Luke 15:1–32.

## REFLECTION

I once gave a retreat to a group of inmates in a women's prison. On Sunday, the prison chaplain was the main celebrant and homilist at mass. I never forgot the point he made to his audience. He took the three stories of the "Lost Sheep," the "Lost Coin" and the "Lost Brother" and told the women that each story is an example of the power of God's love and the joy of being found by the Lord. However, it is much easier to celebrate the return of a lost sheep or a recovered coin because it really doesn't demand much by way of change when the discovery is made.

But it is different when a lost brother or sister returns. It demands a personal change in those at home, and like the brother in the story, they too are frequently angry over all the fuss being paid to the black sheep of the family.

So the prison chaplain told the inmates that by the time they were going home, they would hopefully have changed a great deal. But there would be resentment on the part of some in their homes. Many find it more comfortable to keep one in a box stereotyped as a criminal or jailbird. So he told them not to be discouraged if those at home were not too encouraging and didn't want to take part in any celebration.

The chaplain's insight is true in varying degrees with all of us. How do I cope with change in people that I know? Does their growth challenge my own security? Listen to the questions honestly before you answer in your own heart.

## SHARING

Do I have the same freedom as Moses in communicating with God? Why or why not?

Is my salvation from Christ as real and personal as was Paul's?

From what has the Lord saved me?

Have I grown to the point where I really believe that reconciliation is a celebration of joy and gratitude? What from my experience moves me to answer in this way?

In what specific way will I celebrate another's joy this week?

## ACTION RESPONSE

Choose an action that will enable individuals or the group as a whole to live out in the coming week what has been shared.

## PRAYER

Allow time for spontaneous prayer and close with reading aloud the responsorial psalm of Sunday's liturgy, Psalm 51.

# Twenty-Fifth Sunday of the Year

## OPENING PRAYER

The Alternative Opening Prayer of Today's Liturgy

**READINGS:**        Amos 8:4–7; 1 Timothy 2:1–8; Luke 16:1–13.

## REFLECTION

In a recent book on the church, Avery Dulles has an essay on the abiding significance of Vatican II. He develops ten themes that run throughout the documents. One is that social justice is spoken of, not just as coming from the natural law or abstract reason, but "is a constitutive element of the Gospel." This was the famous formula used by the Bishops' Synod in 1971.

The readings today say a resounding "yes" to that view. Amos represents the theme that runs through all the prophets, which is that justice is one of the chief elements of God's revelation. Amos lists some of the sins against justice and then quotes the Lord "who has sworn never will I forget a thing they have done."

In the gospel, Luke asserts that the other-worldly have to learn from the worldly in dealing with their own kind. He does not proclaim a flight from the world or its goods, but that we must use the world's riches with care and justice. In fact, he says, "If... you are not trustworthy with elusive wealth, who will trust you with true wealth?"

We are bound in justice to use this world's goods wisely and with charity. The important word is "use." We cannot overkill in idolizing goods. Since part of justice is owed to God, we cannot give ourselves to God and to money or wealth. Another case of coupling the serpent's wisdom with the dove's simplicity.

## SHARING

What current sins against justice would Amos speak out against today?

Reread 1 Timothy 2:1–8. Do I think it is possible in today's world to pray without anger or argument?

How can our community respond to the gospel's call to use the world's goods justly and wisely? How can we act upon this call this week?

## ACTION RESPONSE

Choose an action that will enable individuals or the group as a whole to live out in the coming week what has been shared.

## PRAYER

Allow time for spontaneous prayer and close with reading aloud the responsorial psalm of Sunday's liturgy, Psalm 113.

# Twenty-Sixth Sunday of the Year

## OPENING PRAYER

The Alternative Opening Prayer of Today's Liturgy

**READINGS:**  Amos 6:1a, 4–7; 1 Timothy 6:11–16;
Luke 16:19–31.

## REFLECTION

We often read the scriptures exclusively as histories of the past rather than as prophetic insights to the present. Amos is speaking to me and not just to his contemporaries. Paul writes, not just to Timothy, but to every Christian now. Jesus is not just speaking to the Pharisees, but telling a story that should resonate in my heart and be experienced in the present.

How often have we heard the words of Lazarus, "If someone from the dead goes to them, they will repent." But, Jesus retorts, if they don't listen to Moses or the prophets, why should they listen to a nobody like Lazarus or me?

Then Jesus adds a prophetic note. They would not be convinced even "if someone should rise from the dead." Jesus has risen and still we delay in living well before death closes off our time to reform and live. We have to do and be a lot for Christ before the funeral. The word has been spoken in the Old and New Testaments by prophets and by Christ. What further need do we have of any more or better witnesses?

113

## SHARING

Amos warns: "Woe to the complacent in Zion." Where am I most complacent in my life? Where are we most complacent in our small community? What do we ignore? What about in our parish?

In the first sentence of our second reading Paul tells Timothy what he should seek after. In what qualities have we shown the most growth in this past year?

What word of the prophets have I listened to in a way that has changed the quality of my life?

In what specific action this week will I make an effort to remove complacency from my life?

## ACTION RESPONSE

Choose an action that will enable individuals or the group as a whole to live out in the coming week what has been shared.

## PRAYER

Allow time for spontaneous prayer and close with reading aloud the responsorial psalm of Sunday's liturgy, Psalm 146.

# Twenty-Seventh Sunday of the Year

## OPENING PRAYER

The Alternative Opening Prayer of Today's Liturgy

**READINGS:**      Habakkuk 1:2–3; 2:2–4;
2 Timothy 1:6–8, 13–14; Luke 17:5–10.

## REFLECTION

Faith is not the acceptance of abstract truths about God, but rather a wrestling with the mystery of God in our lives. Who has not cried out with Habakkuk, "I cry for help but you do not listen. I cry out to you, 'Violence!' but you do not intervene." The Lord tells me as he does Habakkuk to write down and wait upon the vision and it will surely come. But this is a condition that demands much patience before we can believe that the just person, because of his faith, shall live.

In the same way Paul tells Timothy, "Stir into flame the gift of God that you have through the imposition of my hands." Again, there must be courage and strength to persevere. "For God did not give us a spirit of cowardice but rather of power and love and self-control." It takes courage and strength to wrestle with life and a great deal of patience to wait upon the God who will come. In the meantime, we pray to the Spirit to sustain us, that Spirit who makes us loving and wise.

Luke reminds us that faith is a gift and that we are, at best, faithful servants and stewards of that gift. It is fashionable in our society today to strive to be independent and, above all, to be number one. Therefore, we have to hear at heart level the biblical saying that when we have done all for the Lord "we have done what we were obliged to do." Today's readings remind us that since faith is a gift, it never ceases to be that because we have to wait upon the Lord as servant who responds in strong and courageous faith.

## SHARING

What do I think God meant when he told Habakkuk to "write down the vision" and "wait for it"?

If Paul tells us that "God did not give us a spirit of cowardice," what conclusions can we draw for our service to others?

What is implied in Jesus' statement, "If you have faith the size of a mustard seed..."?

In what specific situations of this coming week will I need to call upon the Spirit who makes me strong, not cowardly?

## ACTION RESPONSE

Choose an action that will enable individuals or the group as a whole to live out in the coming week what has been shared.

## PRAYER

Allow time for spontaneous prayer and close with reading aloud the responsorial psalm of Sunday's liturgy, Psalm 95.

# Twenty-Eighth Sunday of the Year

**OPENING PRAYER**

The Alternative Opening Prayer of Today's Liturgy

**READINGS:**     2 Kings 5:14–17; 2 Timothy 2:8–13;
                  Luke 17:11–19.

**REFLECTION**

To be eucharistic in my prayer and life is literally to be grateful, as the liturgy says, "at all times and places." Constant gratitude leads to deeper faith. That's what both Kings and Luke tell us today.

In Kings, Naaman is a Syrian with leprosy. When Elisha tells him to wash in the Jordan seven times and he is healed, he is filled with gratitude. He moves on from gratitude to faith in the God of Israel. He asks for two mule loads of Israel's earth because it symbolizes for him the holy ground on which God stands. This symbol becomes a reality in his life for from that time on Naaman, too, will stand on holy ground.

In Luke, Jesus heals ten people who have leprosy and sends them on their way to show themselves to the priests. Only one of the ten returns to give thanks and, as in the story of Naaman, he was not an Israelite but a foreigner. When this most unlikely candidate returns, Jesus calls him to deeper healing and to a life–giving journey. "Stand up and go; your faith has saved you."

We who so glory in our eucharistic tradition ought to listen and to practice what the heart of it means. It is to give thanks to you, Lord, at all times and places. Constant gratitude is one of the surest ways of growing in faith. Just ask Naaman and the Samaritan who had leprosy!

## SHARING

Like Naaman, where do we find our holy ground in our parish community?

Is there any word of God that we have chained up in respect to social justice in our community? What is an example of this and what steps can we take to begin a process of unchaining God's word?

Where do I think the other nine people with leprosy went and in what ways do I identify with them?

In what specific way and with whom will I speak words of gratitude this week?

## ACTION RESPONSE

Choose an action that will enable individuals or the group as a whole to live out in the coming week what has been shared.

## PRAYER

Allow time for spontaneous prayer and close with reading aloud the responsorial psalm of Sunday's liturgy, Psalm 98.

# Twenty-Ninth Sunday of the Year

## OPENING PRAYER

The Alternative Opening Prayer of Today's Liturgy

**READINGS:**     Exodus 17:8–13; 2 Timothy 3:14—4:2;
                  Luke 18:1–8.

## REFLECTION

In 1943 Pius XII, through the encyclical, *Divino Afflante Spiritu*, opened our church up to the riches of the word of God with an inspired expectancy that had been missing from the Catholic Church since the Reformation. That beginning bore rich fruit in the work of Vatican II some twenty years later. In our day, the fullness of the word has been restored both in our liturgy and in our spirituality.

We have heard, once again, Paul's advice to Timothy that "you have known [the] sacred scriptures, which are capable of giving you wisdom for salvation through faith in Christ Jesus." Paul charges us to "proclaim the word; be persistent whether it is covenient or inconvenient; convince, reprimand, encourage through all patience and teaching."

This is the word that Moses said is "in your mouths and in your hearts" (Dt 30:14) waiting to be released. This is the word that Jeremiah tried to suppress and then the "burning in his heart" had to be accepted and he spoke again. This is the word spoken on the road to Emmaus that caused the disciples to ask, "Did not our hearts burn within us?" This is the word that must be "pondered in the heart" and eventually become the home that will lead us to "the truth that will set us free."

A woman lector I know always begins on Monday for next

119

Sunday's reading by praying the word each day. On Sunday her proclamation has power. Once after mass she came to me with tear-filled eyes
saying, "Today has been one of the great moments of my life." After
mass a man came to her and thanked her for reading. He told her,
"Today was the first time I ever heard the word of God." Have we
experienced that special day when the word broke into our deepest con-
sciousness? This is the word that will further move us into the holiness
of Jesus. Have we heard the good news of the renewal of the word in
our time?

## SHARING

How does the model of Moses in today's first reading apply to
us as a group to be supportive of one another?

What place does the pondering of the word have in our personal/
communal spirituality?

How do I interpret the last sentence of Luke in today's gospel?

What specific action will I take this week to let the word make
its home in me?

## ACTION RESPONSE

Choose an action that will enable individuals or the group as a
whole to live out in the coming week what has been shared.

## PRAYER

Allow time for spontaneous prayer and close with reading aloud
the responsorial psalm of Sunday's liturgy, Psalm 121.

# Thirtieth Sunday of the Year

**OPENING PRAYER**

The Alternative Opening Prayer of Today's Liturgy

**READINGS:**        Sirach 35:12–14, 16–18; 2 Timothy 4:6–8, 16–18;
                     Luke 18:9–14.

## REFLECTION

Is there not a built-in cumulative guilt by which we as broken people are afraid to approach the perfect God? How dare we? Yet, Sirach almost apologizes in the name of God. God "though not unduly partial toward the weak...hears the cry of the oppressed...the wail of the orphan...the widow when she pours out her complaint."

So, too, does Paul. Having been "poured out like a libation" and in a state where "everyone deserted me," he still has courage to call on the Lord who gives him strength and will continue to rescue him.

Finally, Jesus in the gospel shows where the prejudice of the Father falls. Jesus addresses a parable toward "those who were convinced of their own righteousness and despised everyone else." He contrasts the Pharisee and the tax collector. The first prays out of his own sense of success and good works and, finally, is "good" because the other is so "bad." The tax collector merely says, "O God, be merciful to me a sinner." We are not surprised in this context that Jesus concludes in favor of the second man who "went home justified" while the other did not.

It is hard to believe but it is true nonetheless. We do not come to God to be rewarded for our deeds. But rather, poor and broken, we come to be healed and to be loved.

## SHARING

Let's be honest. Do we ever resent God's partiality toward the weak and broken? Examine why and share.

As I reread Paul's note to Timothy, what are the times in my life when I especially identify with him?

Is there not something of both the Pharisee and the tax collector in all of us? Share examples of both sides.

Do I hold another in contempt? What action will I take to move from contempt to love this week?

## ACTION RESPONSE

Choose an action that will enable individuals or the group as a whole to live out in the coming week what has been shared.

## PRAYER

Allow time for spontaneous prayer and close with reading aloud the responsorial psalm of Sunday's liturgy, Psalm 34.

# Thirty-First Sunday of the Year

## OPENING PRAYER

The Alternative Opening Prayer of Today's Liturgy

**READINGS:**      Wisdom 11:22—12:2; 2 Thessalonians 1:11—2:2;
Luke 19:1–10.

## REFLECTION

The gospel passage today is chapter 19 of Luke. The very next section begins with the entry of Jesus into Jerusalem and introduces us to his passion and death. So this story today is the hinge story on which swings the door to the last and most important part of the life and meaning of Jesus.

The story of Zacchaeus is distilled and abounds with exaggerations that border on irony. How redundant it was to say that he was "a chief tax collector" and "a wealthy man." Imagine that Zacchaeus is the counterpoint of the rich young man who now in his adult alienation comes home to self and to Jesus.

Is his being "short of stature" just a physical limitation or is it the outer expression of the moral and spiritual weakness or shortcoming? His physical size seemed to be no problem when it came to rapping on doors and demanding five or ten shekels as the payment for taxes. In confusion and fear, he goes "up a tree," which we still use as a symbol for confusion in life, and gathers a view of Jesus from where he would be unseen. What a shock and joy it must have been to his little heart to be seen and greeted by name. "Zacchaeus, come down quickly, for today I must stay at your house." He is not bothered by the "theys" and "thems" of his life as he comes down the tree joyfully to greet Jesus. And despite the opposition of "them" who are about him, Zacchaeus "stands his ground" and speaks his words of daring ministry. Jesus refers to it as a special "today," a day that salvation has come to Zacchaeus. We can almost imagine Jesus going home with Zacchaeus and having to stand on tiptoe to put his arm around his shoulder because Zacchaeus had suddenly grown so tall!

## SHARING

From my own experience how would I tackle Wisdom's words, "You rebuke offenders little by little"?

Is there any relevance today to Paul's warning "not to be shaken out of your minds suddenly" or to be alarmed into believing that "the day of the Lord is at hand"? What is the relevance?

How have we as a group "stood our ground" on the things that really matter? What are some examples?

How will I try to see Jesus in my own confusion this coming week?

## ACTION RESPONSE

Choose an action that will enable individuals or the group as a whole to live out in the coming week what has been shared.

## PRAYER

Allow time for spontaneous prayer and close with reading aloud the responsorial psalm of Sunday's liturgy, Psalm 145.

# Thirty-Second Sunday of the Year

## OPENING PRAYER

The Alternative Opening Prayer of Today's Liturgy

**READINGS:**   2 Maccabees 7:1–2, 9–14;
2 Thessalonians 2:16—3:5; Luke 20:27–38.

## REFLECTION

How real is the resurrection for me? Would I have the courage of the seven brothers and suffer torture and death because my new life with God after that is so real? Like the young Maccabees do I live each day in the "God-given hope of being restored to life" by God?

Or, like the Sadducees, am I asking the wrong questions about the future life? Jesus will not even discuss the petty regulations about who will be husband or wife because in the radically new life of the resurrection there will be no marriage. Christ makes it very clear where the bottom line is. Very simply stated, God "is not the God of the dead but of the living." Christ challenges us to live each day in the present and the as yet to be fulfilled resurrection. Jesus tells us in John that if we live and believe, we will never die. That faith and life begin now and that faith is concerned with present life and present belief. The same God of the living (and my life) will not cease being faithful in the life to come after death. It is from this conviction that Paul can say, "Neither death, nor life...will separate us from the love of God in Christ Jesus" (Rom 8:38-39). The acclamation of the liturgy sings of our deep faith that Christ has died and will come again. But for now and forever, "Christ is risen." Our God is still and ever will be a God of the living and of life.

## SHARING

How real is the resurrection for me? Have I ever experienced a "resurrection moment" or a time of being restored to life by God? Share that moment.

How are we as disciples of Christ challenged by life and death issues in our time?

How does our sharing community fulfill Paul's prayer, "May the Lord direct your hearts to the love of God and to the endurance of Christ"?

What is some moment in my journey of the past week wherein I experienced God in my life?

## ACTION RESPONSE

Choose an action that will enable individuals or the group as a whole to live out in the coming week what has been shared.

## PRAYER

Allow time for spontaneous prayer and close with reading aloud the responsorial psalm of Sunday's liturgy, Psalm 17.

# Thirty-Third Sunday of the Year

## OPENING PRAYER

The Alternative Opening Prayer of Today's Liturgy

**READINGS:**    Malachi 3:19–20a; 2 Thessalonians 3:7–12;
Luke 21:5–19.

## REFLECTION

As we come to the end of the liturgical year, the church has us reflect on end time. We consider the end of our own time in the dissolution of death and the end of all time in the dissolution of the world that we have known.

The gospel warns us to be very careful about accepting the predictions of the world's end. There will always be wars, famine and earthquakes somewhere on our planet. But when they will converge as prelude to end time only God knows.

Those current fundamentalists who have the end of the world looming soon would frighten us into a good life. But the real response should be one of joy at the Lord's coming. This is expressed beautifully in the autobiography of St. Thérèse of Lisieux. Plagued by tuberculosis, she awoke one night to feel blood coming from her lips. "I thought I was about to die. I thought my heart would break with joy." Our response should be one of joy whether it is the end of our life or the end of the world.

Another bit of advice against fear is that Jesus tells us not to worry when we are brought up for judgment by unjust magistrates and authorities. "I myself will give you a wisdom in speaking that all your adversaries will be powerless to resent or refute."

Lastly, Jesus tells his contemporaries and us "by perseverance you will secure your lives."

## SHARING

Malachi has fire destroying evil and healing the just. What is some reality or experience which has this double-edged effect in our lives or in the life of this community?

How do I feel about my own death? Have I grown to see it as a joyous prelude to a fuller life? What has helped that growth to happen?

When was there a time in my life when words and wisdom were supplied by the Spirit when I was being judged?

How and with whom will I share my feelings about death this week?

## ACTION RESPONSE

Choose an action that will enable individuals or the group as a whole to live out in the coming week what has been shared.

## PRAYER

Allow time for spontaneous prayer and close with reading aloud the responsorial psalm of Sunday's liturgy, Psalm 98.

# Thirty-Fourth or Last Sunday of the Year (Christ the King)

## OPENING PRAYER

The Alternative Opening Prayer of Today's Liturgy

**READINGS:**     2 Samuel 5:1–3; Colossians 1:12–20;
                  Luke 23:35–43.

## REFLECTION

The readings for the feast of Christ the King hold forth three aspects of the kingship and kingdom of Christ. The Old Testament reading sees Christ in the tradition of King David and stresses the solidarity of the king with his people and the role of shepherd. Christ takes these traits and raises them to a higher level. Christ is one with his body the church and, as the good shepherd, is willing to lay down his life for the sheep.

The second reading from Colossians highlights the kingship of Christ as having a cosmic sweep. Christ the King is the one in whom all creation takes place and by whom all creation is redeemed and centered. All portions of the universe are reconciled in Christ.

The gospel reading stresses yet another side of the kingship of Christ. Throughout his life, Christ always stressed that the kingdom or reign of God was within and among us. His parables told the story time and again that the fullness of this kingdom could be gained at the eleventh hour. Now with the sign, "King of the Jews," on top of the throne of the cross, Jesus extends the kingdom to the good thief. The readings move from an historic model of David, to a cosmic balance of all creation, to a lonely king who can reach out to bring an eleventh hour thief into the reign of God.

## SHARING

In what way does the Davidic model of shepherd console me?

For what one thing or one person would I be willing to lay down my life?

What does the teaching of Colossians say to us as a community called by Vatican II to be "sacrament of the universe"?

How have we as a small community experienced extending our love to the counterparts of the good thief in our society?

What specific action will I take this week "to shepherd" another?

## ACTION RESPONSE

Choose an action that will enable individuals or the group as a whole to live out in the coming week what has been shared.

## PRAYER

Allow time for spontaneous prayer and close with reading aloud the responsorial psalm of Sunday's liturgy, Psalm 122.

# Prayer Resources

---

**(All prayers in this section were written by RENEW staff and volunteers except where noted.)**

## ADVENT/CHRISTMAS SEASON

You spoke and it was made,
She spoke and you were born,
Christ spoke and we were saved,
Speak to us now, God, urgently. Amen.

## LENTEN/EASTER SEASON

Gather us God like fresh cut wheat,
Crush, grind, mill the seed of our souls,
That our body be bread broken and shared. Amen.

Peace was your parting promise,
A peace wrenched from a violent cross.
When our hands are secured on our cross,
May our open arms thus ever offer peace. Amen.

An empty tomb was filled with life,
An unbelieving world was filled with faith,
Fill our desperate hearts with hope,
Our longing with love. Amen.

Ascended Christ,
You did not want to abandon us or leave us orphans,
So you bequeathed your ministry to your church,
Grant us a new Pentecost,
That the driving wind of your love might stir us anew,
And the tongues of fire guide our way. Amen.

**To the Paschal Victim** (Easter)
Christians, to the Paschal Victim
Offer your thankful praises!
A Lamb the sheep redeems:
Christ, who only is sinless,
Reconciles sinners to the Father.
Death and life have contended in
that combat stupendous:
The Prince of life, who died, reigns immortal.
Speak, Mary, declaring
What you saw, wayfaring.
"The tomb of Christ, who is living,
The glory of Jesus' resurrection;
Bright angels attesting,
The shroud and napkin resting.
Yes, Christ my hope is arisen:
To Galilee he goes before you."
Christ indeed from death is risen,
our new life obtaining.
Have mercy, victor King, ever
reigning! Amen. Alleluia
(Taken from *Lectionary for Mass*
Catholic Book Publishing Co.,
New York, 1970.)

**Pentecost Sequence**
Come, Holy Spirit, come!
And from your celestial home
    Shed a ray of light divine!
Come, Father of the poor!
Come, source of all our store!

Come, within our bosoms shine!
You, of comforters the best;
You, the soul's most welcome guest;
Sweet refreshment here below;
In our labor, rest most sweet;
Grateful coolness in the heat;
Solace in the midst of woe.
O most blessed Light divine,
Shine within these hearts of yours,
And our inmost being fill!
Where you are not, people have naught,
Nothing good in deed or thought,
Nothing free from taint of ill.
Heal our wounds, our strength renew;
On our dryness pour your dew;
Wash the stains of guilt away:
Bend the stubborn heart and will;
Melt the frozen, warm the chill;
Guide the steps that go astray.
On the faithful, who adore
And confess you, evermore
In your sev'nfold gift descend;
Give them virtue's sure reward;
Give them your salvation, Lord;
Give them joys that never end.
Amen. Alleluia.
(Adapted from *Lectionary for
Mass* Catholic Book Publishing Co.
New York, 1970.)

## ORDINARY TIME

Creator God, as we gather in your
presence, open our hearts to
your love, open our minds to
seek and see your truth. Help us
to be truly present to each other

and to you as we pray and share
during this time. We ask this in
the presence of Jesus in whose
name we gather. Amen.

God of Our Delight, we come as
we are and we know that you
accept and love us just as we are.
Help us to listen to your Word
and to each other so that we may
become more like you each day. Amen.

Creator, Redeemer, Sanctifier,
create in us a longing for your
love; redeem that within us
which shrinks from your
embrace; sanctify us and help us
overcome all that is not from
you. We make this prayer through
Jesus and in the joy of the Spirit. Amen.

God of All Creation, as the dew
and rain penetrate our earth and
refresh it so let your Word
penetrate our minds and hearts.
Give us a new understanding of
how you want us to be co-
creators with you in our world
today. Amen.

Loving Father, we walk your
earth, we wonder at your sky,
we breathe your air and we
delight in the fire of your love.
Help us to cherish and nourish
this fragile fabric of our
existence which cherishes and
nourishes us. Grant this through

Christ who truly unites heaven
and earth in universal love. Amen.

Giver of all good Gifts, we gather
in your name and give thanks
for all you have been for us and
given us today. May we in turn
share our gifts with each other
and with our sisters and
brothers in need throughout our
world. Teach us, Lord, how to do
this in concrete ways. Amen.

Author of This Book of Life, sow
the seed of your Word into our
hearts that it might germinate
under your care and flower
forth, ripening unto fruits of
charity. In Jesus' name. Amen.

God of all Creation, your beauty
surrounds us each day but
sometimes we fail to see it. Open
our eyes to the beauty of our
universe and the grace of this
moment and let us respond with
a loud Alleluia! Amen.

Amazing God, lure us during our
time together to greater depths
of understanding your wonderful
ways. Keep us aware of the
miracles of life in the midst of
laughter and tears, joys and
sorrows, challenges and pitfalls.
Give us eyes to see you in every
person and event of our lives. Amen.

God of Our Lives, you call us to
be spontaneously alive in your
Spirit. Stir up your Spirit in our
lives and help us respond to
your call in freedom and joy. Amen.

Origin of Every Good, we know
that everything you have
created shares in your glory and
is cherished by your grace. Help
us to glory in, and cheerfully
cherish, our world and each
inhabitant, and thus sense you
author of all. We pray through
Christ and by the power of the
Spirit. Amen.

God of All, sometimes we feel
crushed by the weight of
relationships and setbacks in
our lives. Help us to relax in
your love during this time and
turn our lives over to you
completely. Teach us to give
over to you the burdens we don't
really have to carry. Bless all
those who have caused us any
trouble. Forgive us if we have
been hard on others too. Amen.

Dear Father,
How wonderful are those words!
We know that we can only say
them because of your tremendous
love for us. You sent us the
WORD—Jesus!
He told us about you, and our
companion Holy Spirit. As we your children gather here,

we are grateful for those who
have loved us with your love.
We deeply desire to continue to
love each other and those you
allow to come into our lives with
the power of your love. Amen.

Thank you, God, for loving us
into new life each day. Give us a
greater appreciation of who you
really are in our lives and who
we really are and can be for one
another. Amen.

Father, you awaken in us each
day small ways to be faithful to
you. Prod us along and be
patient with us. We want to
respond with all our hearts.
Teach us how! We ask this in
Jesus' name. Amen.

Hello God, we gather again in your
presence and desire to cast all our
anxieties and cares into your
loving arms. Take them now so
we can be free to hear you in the
Word proclaimed. Help us in our
feeble attempts to respond to your
Word. Amen.

Lord Jesus, you are the vine, we
are the branches.
Help us to always be attached to
you that our lives may bear fruit.
Be with us today (this evening) as
we share your Word and how it
touches our life. Amen.

We have come together, Lord
Jesus, to listen to your word in
scripture and in the story of our
lives. Open us to your love and to
one another so we may be wiser,
gentler, freer. Amen.

**The Memorare**
Remember, O most gracious Virgin
Mary, that never was it known
that anyone who fled to your
protection, implored your help, or
sought your intercession, was left
unaided. Inspired by this
confidence, I fly unto you, O virgin
of virgins, my Mother. To you I
come; before you I stand sinful
and sorrowful. O Mother of the
Word Incarnate! Despise not my
petitions, but in your mercy hear
and answer me. Amen.
(Attributed to St. Bernard)

**Mary, the Evangelist**
O Mary, you were the first
Christian evangelist. By God's
invitation through the angel
Gabriel and by your free choice
you accepted Jesus into your life.
By giving birth to Jesus you gifted
us with our most wonderful
brother and friend and savior.
Thank you, Mary, for being with
the apostles when you welcomed
the Holy Spirit who empowered all
of you to evangelize the world.
Pray that the same Holy Spirit will
empower us today to be good

evangelizers. Be our mother and
mediatrix today, Mary. Amen.

## RENEW Prayer to Mary

Mary, you are a woman
wrapped in silence
and yet the Word
born of your yes
continues to bring life
to all creation.
Mary, help us to say yes—
to be bearers of good news
to a world waiting.

Mary, you are a virgin
and a mother
empowered by the Holy Spirit.
Help us to open ourselves
to that same life-bringing Spirit.
Mary, help us to say our yes.

Mary, you are gift of Jesus to us,
mother of the church.
Look upon our world
and our lives.
Pray for us to your Son
that we might be renewed
that we might help renew
the face of the earth.
Mary, help us to say yes. Amen.

## Prayer of St. Francis of Assisi

Lord, make me an instrument of your peace:
where there is hatred, let me sow love;
where there is injury, pardon;
where there is doubt, faith;
where there is despair, hope;
where there is darkness, light;

and where there is sadness, joy.
O, Divine Master, grant that I may not so much seek
to be consoled as to console,
to be understood as to understand,
to be loved as to love.
For it is in giving that we receive,
it is in pardoning that we are pardoned,
and it is in dying that we are born to eternal life.
(Attributed to Francis of Assisi)

## Prayer for RENEW
LORD, We are your people,
    the sheep of your flock.
Heal the sheep who are wounded,
Touch the sheep who are in pain,
Clean the sheep who are soiled,
Warm the lambs who are cold.

Help us to know the Father's love
    through Jesus the shepherd
    and through the Spirit.
Help us to lift up that love,
    and show it all over this land.
Help us to build love on justice
    and justice on love.
Help us to believe mightily,
    hope joyfully,
    love divinely.

Renew us that we may help renew
    the face of the earth. Amen.

# *Suggested Action Responses*

---

The most effective actions are usually not projects separate from everyday life but the integration of our Christian conviction in our family life, work, recreation and places of activity. Therefore, the most appropriate action is usually one very unique to the individual that is connected with the circumstances and challenges of everyday life. Changing the environment or society in which we live is probably the most valuable way of putting faith in practice.

When this type of action step is not immediately evident it is worth considering projects that are connected with our sharing and may be particularly timely. The following suggestions are not intended to limit imagination but to aid creativity especially when the action response is aimed toward a project.

Visit elderly, shut-ins, prisoners, sick.

Provide transportation to elderly and disabled for doctor's visits, grocery shopping, community activities, church.

Organize people to come together to work on community problems (i.e., drugs, crime, unsafe neighborhoods).

Provide cultural activities for disadvantaged youth.

Stock food banks and provide food baskets.

Become involved in organizations such as Bread for the World, Habitat for Humanity, Amnesty International, Pax Christi.

Start a food co-op in your area.

Work with youth groups to organize a neighborhood or community clean-up project.

Work in soup kitchens.

Protest to advertisers or television stations regarding the following: violence, sexual promiscuity, vulgar language, inappropriate role models for children and teenagers, and making fun of cruelty to animals.

Plant a vegetable garden and share some of your harvest with others in need.

Provide clothing to clothing centers.

Work ecumenically to open food banks and soup kitchens.

Assist with Meals on Wheels to be effective in the local area.

Staff emergency assistance centers.

Assist at homeless shelters.

Set up shelters for the homeless or provide parish resources for housing the homeless.

Educate children about our dependence on each other and on the natural world.

Paint homes for disadvantaged people.

Recycle bottles, cans, plastic, paper, clothes.

Work with municipal and state authorities to implement recycling programs or centers.

Provide furniture for those in need.

Visit nursing homes and provide needed care and support.

Host rummage sales where profits are used for the needy.

Gather baby clothes for young pregnant teens or teen moms.

Buy recycled products; reuse grocery bags.

Share with and support terminally ill people.

Clean-up campaigns for neighborhood parks.

Sponsor ecumenical social activities to bring people together to celebrate special occasions.

Join community-based groups that work to conserve resources, to save and protect the environment.

Have a simple vegetarian meal once a week; donate your savings to an appropriate cause.

Help with literacy needs in the community.

Tutor those with special educational needs.

Help with voter registration.

Write a letter to a prisoner or someone in a hospital or nursing home.

Write letters to leaders in Congress regarding concerns for the poor and disadvantaged or to address community needs (i.e., housing needs).

Take a nature walk and reflect on your connectedness with all of creation.

Organize neighborhoods for community improvements addressing total community needs, particularly neighborhood housing needs.

Save energy: adequately insulate your home; turn off lights and appliances when appropriate.

Do without unnecessary appliances, e.g., electric can-openers, knives, etc.

Attend a local city government and school board meeting and encourage community values.

Walk, bicycle, car pool, use public transportation.

Be a voice for the poor and homeless at community meetings.

Try to live more simply so that resources can be distributed more equally.